BELOVED BRIDE

Beloved Bride

THE LETTERS OF STONEWALL JACKSON TO HIS WIFE

1857-1863

WILLIAM POTTER

THE VISION FORUM, INC.
SAN ANTONIO, TEXAS

To Leslie, my loving esposa

CONTENTS

FOREWORD

The mists of legend swirl thickly around our nation's memory of Thomas Jonathan "Stonewall" Jackson. There is, of course, a certain attraction in obscurity, for it allows us, indeed requires us, to see the Jackson we want to see, the Jackson that most neatly suits our own particular historical agenda. It is strange that our view of Jackson should be thus, for so much has been written about Jackson, and accurately written at that. Diaries, memoirs, battle reports, letters, and testimonials paint a specific and multilayered portrait of a major protagonist in the national tragedy that was the Civil War. To understand that war, to appreciate the reasons and passions behind it, it is necessary to penetrate the mists of legend and see the man clearly in all his aspects.

Any portrait of Jackson would be woefully incomplete without giving full understanding to the depth of his love for Anna Morrison Jackson. Such a portrait would be missing his heart. The Thomas-Anna relationship is not merely the conventional woman behind the man, the "General's General" as it were, but a central and vital web in the tapestry of his soul. Anna did not just support Jackson, although she did that. She did not just enable Jackson, although she did that. She did not just provide him emotional sustenance, although she assuredly did that. For Jackson, Anna was a living and breathing example of God's goodness and beneficence, of the absolute beauty of life on this earth, of the piece of God's plan that allowed for happiness and fulfillment in this life. Anna not only shared his faith, she epitomized his faith, she sweetened his faith, she completed his faith. Through his relationship with Anna his relationship with God was enriched, deepened, and widened from the concept of an all-powerful God of justice and ultimate judgment to a God of love. Without Anna, Jackson may well have hardened into the unbending ascetic many believe him to have been. They are mistaken. Her presence in his life brought balance. Her influence and guidance did not inhibit the qualities that made "Stonewall" Jackson a warrior among warriors, but greatly enhanced the virtues that made Thomas Jackson a man among men.

Stephen Lang
September 18, 2002

Mr. Lang brings his brilliant and never-to-be-surpassed portrayal of General Jackson to the Ron Maxwell film, *Gods and Generals*.

ACKNOWLEDGEMENTS

Special thanks to director and producer Ron Maxwell for his encouragement for this book and permission to use the cover images of Mr. and Mrs. Jackson from his film *Gods and Generals*. The remarkable portrayal for the silver screen by actor Stephen Lang of Stonewall Jackson as a Christian man and husband is sure to inspire untold thousands to learn more about the greatest Christian general in the history of this nation. I am thankful that God has worked through director Maxwell to produce such a courageous and never-to-be-forgotten film. Thanks also to James Robertson, the greatest of all biographers of the General, for bringing Jackson scholarship to a new height. Posthumous gratitude is extended to my great hero, Robert Louis Dabney, who painstakingly chronicled the life of Jackson a century ago and published many of his letters and private correspondences, as well as to Lloyd Sprinkle who has educated an entire generation through his commitment to republish Dabney's works. Eternal thanks for my own beloved *esposa*, Leslie, whose patience and encouragement of me springs eternal and who served alongside me with joy through many hours of typing and research.

JACKSON, THE MAN

Confederate General Thomas Jonathan Jackson achieved world-wide renown for wielding his army as a champion fencer would his rapier, making bold tactical thrusts when least expected, parrying his enemy's counterstrokes, and finally wrecking the plans of an arrogant and more powerful opponent. Generations of readers of American military history have thrilled at his Virginia brigade's stand at the Battle of First Manassas where his unflinching courage and self-control decided the battle at the crucial moment. He came away from that fight forever after renamed "Stonewall" Jackson.

They also wonder in amazement at his audacious and ingenious Shenandoah Valley Campaign, where three separate Union armies were bamboozled, lured into unfavorable terrain, and brought to grief through hard marching and relentless attack. General Jackson's stand at II Manassas again showed his mettle as his out-of-ammunition and decimated regiments repelled the final enemy attacks by throwing rocks at them. At Chancellorsville in May of 1863, Stonewall Jackson fought his most magnificent battle and was mortally wounded on a late night patrol near enemy lines.

What those who only study military campaigns may not know is that the mighty warrior, the indefatigable leader, the paragon of duty and obedience was also a godly Christian husband and father, a man devoted to the Lord Jesus Christ, and a humble saint determined to live by biblical precepts. Pastor Moses Hoge, who knew him well, recorded that "to portray the life of Jackson while leaving out the religious elements, would be like undertaking to describe Switzerland without mention of the Alps."

As a member of the Lexington Presbyterian Church before the war, Major Jackson faithfully served as a deacon, taught a Sabbath school, and adorned the Gospel of Christ in all his activities whether as professor at the Virginia Military Institute or as the devoted husband of his precious Mary Anna. His beginnings, however, contained no hint of future fame or of the devout testimony that his life would evince through the Providence of God.

Born of Scotch-Irish heritage in the rugged mountains of northwestern Virginia in 1824, Thomas Jackson, at age three, witnessed the deaths of his older sister and his father, who left his grieving widow with no property or livelihood. Thomas' mother died four years later, and he went to live with his Uncle Cummins, who taught him farming and milling and to live by an independent and self-reliant spirit. Thomas developed character traits in his early years that would enable him to face difficult learning situations later in life. He was known for his self-control and for being "one of those untiring, plain, matter-of-fact persons who would never give up . . . until he accomplished his object." He was well known for his honesty and exhibited a youthful interest in religion.

In 1842, armed with recommendations from local citizens who praised his moral character, Thomas J. Jackson received an appointment from his congressman to enter the United States Military Academy at West Point, New York. Lacking the social graces, fashionable attire, and careless humor of most of his classmates, Jackson was not included in the friendship circles, which included such future generals in the War Between the States as A.P. Hill, George B. McClellan, and George Pickett. The older, more mature Jackson did make warm friendships with several upperclassmen. Known for being shy, impassive, and aloof, Jackson paid little attention to anything other than his lessons. In four years of painful and persevering study and physical exercise, Thomas Jackson earned the respect of his peers and finished seventeenth out of fifty-nine graduating cadets in 1846. "More than one observer was convinced that had the West Point curriculum lasted another year, the pitifully prepared mountain boy of 1842 would have graduated at the top of his class." [1]

As a newly brevetted second lieutenant of artillery, Jackson joined Winfield Scott's expedition to fight in the War with Mexico. Lt. Jackson's service in the war, especially at Chapultepec, resulted in dispatches describing his conspicuous gallantry and prompt obedience to orders. He had, in fact, shown fearlessness in the face of overwhelming Mexican fire directed at his battery and had led his men in one of the most heroic actions of the war. The occasion of the War with Mexico was personally important for one other major reason. His friend Captain Francis Taylor encouraged him to fully commit to Christ as his Lord and Savior, and in response, Lt. Jackson cast aside all of his former reluctance and excuses and devoted his life to seeking the glory of God and obedience to biblical precepts.

Following the war, Jackson served in several uninspiring posts and experienced a decline in health. In 1852, at the age of 27, he resigned from the army to accept a teaching position at the Virginia Military Institute in Lexington, Virginia, thus embarking on a new career in a place that providentially would lead to spiritual maturity and service among God's flock in that city and to a loving and faithful marriage. Thomas Jackson's dedication to God was total and unswerving; the first resolution he made regarding his goal to love God fully was to "never violate the known will of God." Among his first purchases after openly professing Christ and joining the Lexington Presbyterian Church was a copy of the Bible which he read daily and underlined favorite passages like Romans 8: 28, "And we know that all things work together for good to them that love God, to them who are the called according to his purpose." He helped found the Rockbridge Bible Society and over the years contributed both time and money in an effort to get God's Word into the hands of everyone in the county.

Jackson sought to keep the Sabbath day holy and would inculcate the practice of Sabbath-keeping with his wife and servants. Worship, rest, Bible reading, and meditation on the glories of Christ were the order of the day. He, in fact, would not mail a letter if he thought it would travel on Sunday. As his pastor William S. White observed, "His faith ... not only made him brave, but gave form, order, direction and power to his whole life."

Major Jackson was well known as a man of prayer; no matter was too small to bring before God. Once he told his sister-in-law, "I have so fixed the habit in my mind that I never raise a glass of water to my lips without a moment's asking for God's blessing. I never seal a letter without putting a word of prayer under the seal. I never take a letter from the post without a brief sending of my thoughts heavenward. I never change my classes in the section room without a minute's petition on the cadets who go out and those who come in."

Among Jackson's acquaintances was the Rev. George Junkin, D.D., the president of Washington College and a well-known Old School Presbyterian evangelist and preacher with whom he discussed various topics of interest, especially theology. In due course, Jackson developed an intense love for Dr. Junkin's youngest daughter, Elinor, a beautiful, vivacious, and godly young woman. The rather stiff and formal ex-army officer secretly courted Ellie for about six months before they were joined in marriage by her father in his home in August of 1853.

Thomas Jackson had never known such love and companionship, and he was thoroughly enraptured by his beloved Ellie. One of Jackson's biographers has observed that "the new Mrs. Jackson possessed an orderliness grounded in love and faith that gave her a tranquility he had never had without laboring for it. It was Ellie who drew him from his shell of shyness. She joked with him, took him to new places, substituted affectionate companionship for the lonely evenings he had endured. Jackson became more relaxed and more open . . . [he] was happier than he had ever been." [2]

Thomas Jackson's joyous life with Ellie ended abruptly on October 22, 1854. She gave birth to a stillborn son and followed him to the grave within the hour. In his compounded grief, Jackson's faith in God's mercy sustained him. In a letter to his sister he wrote:

> I have been called to pass through the deep waters of affliction, but all has been satisfied. The Lord giveth and the Lord taketh away, blessed be the name of the Lord. It is his will that my Dearest wife & child should no longer abide with me, and as it is his holy will, I am perfectly reconciled to the sad bereavement, though I deeply mourn my loss. Oh! The consolations of religion! I can willingly submit to anything if God strengthens me. I have joy in knowing that God withholds no good things from them that love and keep his commandments. And he will overrule this Sad, Sad bereavement for good.

Over the next two years, Major Jackson attended to duties at the military institute, traveled through Europe visiting culturally important sites, continued local business activity, and served faithfully as a teacher in the church. He also turned his attentions to a girl from North Carolina whom he had met years earlier when she visited her married sister in Lexington. Mary Anna Morrison believed as Jackson did that all events of a person's life were links in a chain of providence, fulfilling God's ultimate purposes. Of that seeming inconsequential visit to her sister, Anna later remarked, "Of course I cannot but look upon it as a special providence that led me there to meet him who was to be my future husband."

Mary Anna Morrison was the third of six daughters of the patriarchal Robert Hall Morrison, a Presbyterian pastor with ten children. According to a family friend, Anna was fair in person, beautiful in character, amiable and loving by nature, intelligent, cultivated, refined, and pious. The quiet and respectful professor from VMI visited the Morrison home near Charlotte in December 1856, and thus began a friendship which became courtship in a few months and a wedding on July 16, 1857. Thomas Jackson's marriage to Mary Anna Morrison would last but six years, yet their personal relationship, their home life, their godly testimony to the church and the community would continue to inspire and teach Christian families until today.

Chapter 1

COURTSHIP AND MARRIAGE

Stonewall Jackson began writing his tender and instructive letters to his wife during their courtship and continued regularly whenever they were apart, until days before his death in 1863. Mary Anna recorded in *The Life and Letters of Stonewall Jackson* that her husband "was a great advocate for marriage, appreciating the gentler sex so highly that whenever he met one of the 'unappropriated blessings' under the type of truest womanhood, he would wish that one of his bachelor friends could be fortunate to win her." She noted that the letters she received during their engagement revealed the "tenderness of his nature, and how with this human affection were mingled a boundless love and gratitude to Him who was the giver of all."

General Jackson's letters to his wife were most likely destroyed by her before her death in 1915. Nevertheless, in

1891 she published extracts of his correspondence to her to the great delight and benefit of all who have read them.

The first letter was written sometime in April 1857 from his home in Lexington to his affianced Mary Anna Morrison living in her family's homestead, Cottage Home, in North Carolina. Anna's sister Isabella was married to Major Daniel Harvey Hill, a professor at Davidson College and future Major General in the Confederate army. He was a close friend of Major Jackson and the death of Hill's infant son came as a hard blow to the family.

> *APRIL 1857* I wrote to Major and Mrs. Hill a few days since, and my prayer is that this heavy affliction may be sanctified to them. I was not surprised that little MC was taken away, as I have long regarded his father's attachment to him as too strong; that is, so strong that he would be unwilling to give him up, though God should call for his own. I do not believe that an attachment ever is, or can be, absolutely too strong for any object of our affections; but our love to God may not be strong enough. We may not love Him so intensely as to have no will but His. . . . Is there not a comfort in prayer which is nowhere else to be found?

Major Jackson wrote at least four more letters to his betrothed prior to their wedding on July 16, 1857.

> *APRIL 25, 1857* It is a great comfort to me to know that although I am not with you, yet you are in the hands of

One who will not permit any evil to come nigh you. What a consoling thought it is to know that we may, with perfect confidence, commit all our friends in Jesus to the care of our Heavenly Father, with an assurance that all will be well with them! . . . I have been sorely disappointed at not hearing from you this morning, but these disappointments are all designed for our good.

In my daily walks I think much of you. I love to stroll abroad after the labors of the day are over, and indulge feelings of gratitude to God for all the sources of natural beauty with which he has adorned the earth. Some time since, my morning walks were rendered very delightful by the singing of the birds. The morning carolling of the birds, and their sweet notes in the evening, awaken in me devotional feelings of praise and thanksgiving, though very different in their nature. In the morning, all animated nature (man excepted) appears to join in expressions of gratitude to God; in the evening, all is hushing into silent slumber, and thus disposes the mind to meditation. And as my mind dwells on you, I love to give it a devotional turn, by thinking of you as a gift from our Heavenly Father.

How delightful it is thus to associate every pleasure and enjoyment with God the Giver!

Thus will He bless us, and make us grow in grace, and in the knowledge of Him, whom to know aright is life eternal.

MAY 7, 1857 I wish I could be with you to-morrow at your communion. Though absent in body, yet in spirit I shall be present, and my prayer will be for your growth in every Christian grace.... I take special pleasure in the part of my prayers in which I beg that every temporal and spiritual blessing may be yours, and that the glory of God may be the controlling and absorbing thought of our lives in our new relation. It is to me a great satisfaction to feel that our Heavenly Father has so manifestly ordered our union. I believe, and am persuaded, that if we but walk in His commandments, acknowledging Him in all our ways, he will shower His blessings upon us. How delightful it is to feel that we have such a friend, who changes not! The Christian's recognition of God in all His works greatly enhances his enjoyment.

MAY 16, 1857 There is something very pleasant in the thought of your mailing me a letter every Monday; such manifestation of regard for the Sabbath must be well-pleasing in the sight of God. Oh that all our people would manifest such a regard for his holy day! If we would all strictly observe his holy laws, what would not our country be? ... When in prayer for you last Sabbath, the tears came to my eyes, and I realized an unusual degree of emotional tenderness. I have not yet fully analyzed my feelings to my satisfaction, so as to arrive at the cause of such emotions; but I am disposed to think that it consisted in the idea of the intimate relation existing between you, as the object of my tender affection, and God, to whom I looked up as my Heavenly Father. I felt that day as if it were a communion day for myself.

JUNE 20, 1857 I never remember to have felt so touchingly as last Sabbath the pleasure springing from the thought of prayers ascending for my welfare from one tenderly beloved. There is something very delightful in such spiritual communion.

Anna wrote that her father "could not trust his emotional nature enough to marry any of his daughters," so the Rev. Dr. Drury Lacy performed the ceremony at the Morrison home. During the war Dr. Lacy preached many times to the Confederate troops and became General Jackson's de facto headquarters chaplain.

Chapter Two

NEWLYWEDS

The newlyweds established their home about a half-mile from the Virginia Military Institute and settled into true domestic tranquility. The straight-laced professor proved quite a different sort at home. Anna wrote that "in his home no man could have been more unrestrained and demonstrative, and his buoyancy and sportiveness were quite a revelation to me when I became a sharer in the privacy of his inmost life. These demonstrations and playful endearments he kept up as long as he lived; time seemed to intensify instead of diminish them."

The Jackson's first child, Mary Graham, arrived on April 30, 1858. The ledger of a local merchant recorded that the Major purchased a crib and hair mattress on May 12 and "one fine cloth, coffin, and box" on May 26 for little Mary had died of jaundice the day before. Anna later recorded that the baby's death was a "great, very great sorrow" to him but he spent his time ministering to her for "he was the most tender, affectionate, demonstrative man, . . . [and] he was full of love and gentleness."

In the spring of 1859, Mrs. Jackson fell ill and her husband determined that the best medical attention could be found in New York. She had to remain there for several weeks but he returned to his duties at the Institute. Their first separation brought frequent letters from Lexington to New York though only parts of three of them have survived. We find in these letters his pet name for her, *esposa*, reminiscent of his days in Mexico and his enjoyment of the Spanish language. He also mentions three of the six slaves in the Jackson household— Amy, Hetty, and George. Forty-four-year-old Amy cooked and cleaned house. Hetty had been Anna's nurse since infancy and was given to her as a wedding gift by her father. George was one of Hetty's teenage sons whom Anna taught to read.

MARCH 1859   I got home last night in as good health as when I gave my darling the last kiss. Hetty and Amy came to the door when I rang, but would not open until I gave my name. They made much ado about my not bringing you home. Your husband has a sad heart. Our house looks so deserted without my *esposa*. Home is not home without my little dove. I love to talk to you, little one, as though you were here, and tell you how much I love you, but that will not give you the news. . . . During our absence the servants appear to have been faithful, and I am well pleased with the manner in which they discharged their duties. George came to me to-day, saying he had filled all the wood-boxes,

and asked permission to go fishing, which was granted. . . .
You must be cheerful and happy, remembering that you are
somebody's sunshine.

APRIL 27, 1859   All your fruit-trees are yielding fruit this
year. When George brought home your cow this morning,
she was accompanied by one fine little representative of his
sire, and it would do your heart good to see your big cow
and your little calf, and to see what a fine prospect there
is for an abundant supply of milk. . . . We had lettuce for
dinner to-day from your hot-bed. Heretofore I have been
behind Captain Hayden's calendar for gardening, which
he wrote out for me; but this day brings me up with it,
and I hope hereafter to follow it closely. I have arranged
under each month its programme for the different days, so
I have but to look at the days of the month, and follow its
directions as then come.

MAY 7, 1859   I received only three letters last week, and
have only one so far this week, but 'hope springs eternal in
the human breast;' so you see I am becoming quite poetical
since listening to a lecture on the subject last evening. . . . I
send you a flower from your garden, and could have sent one
in full bloom, but I thought this one, which is just opening,
would be in a better state of preservation when my little
dove receives it. You must not give yourself any concern
about your *esposo's* living. . . . My little pet, your husband
was made very happy at receiving two letters from you and

learning that you were improving so rapidly. I have more than once bowed down on my knees, and thanked our kind and merciful Heavenly Father for the prospect of restoring you to health again. Now, don't get impatient, and come off before you are entirely well.... Yesterday Doctor Junkin preached one of his masterly sermons on the sovereignty of God, and, although a doctrinal discourse, it was eminently consoling; and I wish that you could have heard such a presentation of the subject. To-day I rode your horse out to your lot and saw your laborers. They are doing good work. I was mistaken about your large garden fruit being peaches, they turn out to be apricots; and just think—my little woman has a tree full of them! You must come home before they get ripe. You have the greatest show of flowers I have seen this year. Enclosed are a few specimens. Our potatoes are coming up. We have had very uncommonly dry weather for nearly a fortnight, and your garden had been thirsting for rain till last evening, when the weather commenced changing and to-day we have had some rain. Through grace given me from above, I felt that the rain would come at the right time, and I don't recollect having ever felt so grateful for rain as for the present one.... You must not be discouraged at the slowness of recovery. Look up to Him who giveth liberally for faith to be resigned to His divine will, and trust Him for that measure of health which will most glorify Him and advance to the greatest extent your own real happiness. We are sometimes suffered to be in a state of perplexity, that our faith may be tried and grow stronger. 'All things work together for good' to God's children. See if you cannot spend a short time after dark in looking out of your window into space, and meditating upon heaven, with all its joys unspeakable and full of glory; and think of what the Saviour relinquished in glory when he came to earth, and of his sufferings for us; and seek to realize, with the apostle, that the afflictions of the present life are not worthy to be compared with the glory which shall be revealed in us. Try to look up and be cheerful, and not desponding. Trust our kind Heavenly Father, and by the eye of faith see that all things with you are right and for your best interest. The clouds come, pass over us, and are followed by bright sunshine; so, in God's moral dealings with us, he permits us to have trouble awhile. But let us, even in the most trying dispensations of His providence, be cheered by the brightness which is a little ahead. Try to live near to Jesus, and secure that peace which flows like a river. You have your husband's prayers, sympathy, and love.

I am so glad and thankful that you received the draft and letters in time. How kind is God to His children! I feel so thankful to Him that He has blessed me with so much faith, though. I well know that I have not that faith which it is my privilege to have. But I have been taught never to despair, but to wait, expecting the blessing at the last moment. Such occurrences should strengthen our faith in Him who never slumbers. . . . I trust that our Heavenly Father is restoring my darling to health, and that when she gets home she will again be its sunshine. Your husband is looking forward with great joy to seeing her bright little face in her own home once more. If you should be detained longer, I will send you some summer clothing, but get everything that is necessary there. I sent you a check in order that you may have ample funds. I know how embarrassing it is even to anticipate scarcity of money when one is away from home.

You are one darling of darlings, and may our kind and merciful Heavenly Father bless you with speedy restoration to health and to me, and with every needful blessing, both temporal and spiritual, is my oft-repeated prayer. Take good care of my little dove, and remember that the day of miracles is past, and that God works by means, and He punishes us for violating his physical as well as His moral laws. When you come home, I want to meet you at Goshen in a private conveyance, and bring my little one gently over the rough roads. I hope you will take my advice, and not burden yourself by carrying anything in your hands, except your umbrella and basket. You are very precious to somebody's heart, if you are away off in New York. My heart is with my *exposita* all the time, and my prayers are for her safety.

How I wish you were here now to share with me the pleasures of home, our garden, and the surrounding country, which is clothed in verdure and beauty! ... On Wednesday your *esposo* hopes to meet his sunshine, and may he never see its brightness obscured, nor its brilliancy diminished by spots!

Chapter Three
TRAVELS

During the summer of 1859, both Anna and Thomas experienced health problems, and he decided that the best cure would be to visit the mineral springs. Many Virginians of the nineteenth century believed in the curative powers of the mountain waters where entrepreneurs established hotels and cabins to accommodate the visitors. Believing the White Sulphur Springs trip too arduous for his wife, he traveled there by himself while she visited the Rockbridge Alum nearer their home. While there, Major Jackson heard a sermon by James Henley Thornwell, one of the greatest Southern Presbyterian preachers of the century.

> *JULY 1859*   This is a very beautiful place, and I wish very much that I had my dove here. I feel that I must bring her here sometime. She would enjoy it greatly, and I should enjoy it so much more if she were with me. To-morrow, you know, was my day to write, but I thought I would drop

you a line to-day, so that you might know the whereabouts of your husband. . . . I am tired of this place, and wouldn't give my little pet for all the people here. I want to go and stay with my little woman. As yet I am not certain whether the waters are beneficial to me.

AUGUST 15, 1859   Last night I enjoyed what I have long desired—listening to a sermon from the Rev. Dr. Thornwell, of South Carolina. He opened with an introduction, setting forth the encouragements and discouragements under which he spoke. Among the encouragements, he stated that the good effected here would be widely disseminated, as there were visitors from every Southern State. Following the example of the apostle Paul, he observed that whilst he felt an interest in all, yet he felt a special interest in those from his own State. He spoke of the educated and accomplished audience it was his privilege to address. After concluding his introductory remarks, he took his text from Genesis, seventeenth chapter, seventh verse, which he presented in a bold, profound, and to me original manner. I felt what a privilege it was to listen to such an exposition of God's truth. He showed that in Adam's fall we had been raised from the position of servants to that of children of God. He gave a brief account of his own difficulties when a college student, in comprehending his relation to God. He represented man as a redeemed being at the day of judgment, standing nearest to the throne, the angels being farther removed. And why? Because his Brother is sitting upon the throne he is a nearer relation to Christ than the angels. And his being the righteousness of God himself. I don't recollect having ever before felt such love to God. I was rather surprised at seeing so much grace and gesture in Dr. Thornwell. I hope and pray that much good will result from this great exposition of Bible truth. . . . Early yesterday morning the tables in the parlor were well supplied with religious tracts. . . . Time passes more pleasantly here than expected, but I want to get back to my *esposita*, and I never want to go to any watering-place without her again.

In September of the same year, Anna visited her father in North Carolina and received, in part, the following letters from Thomas. Anna recorded that he hoped she was feeling "as lively as a lark" and "as happy as a spring butterfly."

SEPTEMBER 1859 I am writing at my desk, which I have raised so high that it makes me stand straight. I watered your flowers this morning, and hoed another row of turnips, and expect to hill some of the celery this evening. Your old man at home is taking good care of one somebody's flower-slips, and they are looking very nicely. Yesterday I went into the kitchen and sealed some jars of tomatoes, and Hetty has put up many jars besides, of plums and other fruits, so that we shall be well supplied this winter. I hope they will keep well. . . . I was invited a few days since to go to the Misses B——'s and see some pagan idols which they had received. They were mostly paintings and some other devices, but quite interesting. Among the various Chinese curiosities (for they do not all refer to worship) was an image consisting of a man in miniature in a sitting posture, with long ringlets of hair hanging from various parts of the face. The statue can be removed from the chair in which it sits, and is the best-finished piece of workmanship of the kind that I ever saw from a pagan land. It was taken from one of the churches in Canton after its capture, and is said to have been worshipped. "I hope that my little somebody is feeling as lively as a lark."

OCTOBER 17, 1859   I have been wishing that you could see our beautiful forests in their autumnal glory. I have been greatly enjoying their beauty, but my pleasure would be much enhanced if you were here with me. I have just been thinking how happy you must be in your old home, and it makes my heart happy too to think of the happiness of my little darling.

Chapter Four

THE CALM BEFORE THE STORM

In October the terrorist John Brown, financed by a cabal of New England radical abolitionists unleashed an attack on Virginia at the arsenal town of Harper's Ferry about 150 miles down the Shenandoah Valley from Lexington. Determined to incite a slave insurrection and establish a mountain stronghold for his growing army, Brown's nineteen killers were trapped in the firehouse where most were killed or captured by United States Marines. Old Brown was convicted of murder and treason against Virginia and sentenced to be hanged in Charles Town.

Governor Henry Wise called on the cadets of the Virginia Military Institute to help provide security in the event that more abolitionist desperadoes might stage a rescue. Major Jackson's letters take on the tone of a soldier on duty.

NOVEMBER 28, 1859, CHARLESTOWN I reached here last night in good health and spirits. Seven of us slept in the same room. I am much pleased than I expected to be; the people appear to be very kind. There are about one thousand troops here, and everything is quiet so far. We don't expect any trouble. The excitement is confined to more distant points. Do not give yourself any concern about me. I am comfortable, for a temporary military post.

DECEMBER 2, 1859 John Brown was hung to-day at about half-past eleven A.M. He behaved with unflinching firmness. The arrangements were well made and well executed under the direction of Colonel Smith. The gibbet was erected in a large field, southeast of the town. Brown rode on the head of his coffin from his prison to the place of execution. The coffin was of black walnut, enclosed in a box of poplar of the same shape as the coffin. He was dressed in a black frock-coat, black pantaloons, black vest, black slouch hat, white socks, and slippers of predominating red. There was nothing around his neck but his shirt collar. The open wagon in which he rode was strongly guarded on all sides. Captain Williams (formerly assistant professor at the Institute) marched immediately in front of the wagon. The jailer, high-sheriff, and several others rode in the same wagon with the prisoner. Brown had his arms tied behind him, and ascended the scaffold with apparent cheerfulness. After reaching the top of the platform, he shook hands with several who were standing around him. The sheriff placed the rope around his neck, then threw a white cap over his head, and asked him if he wished a signal when all should be ready. He replied that it made no difference, provided he was not kept waiting too long. In this condition he stood for about ten minutes of the trap-door, which was supported on one side by hinges and on the other (the south side) by a rope. Colonel Smith then announced to the sheriff "all ready"—which apparently was not comprehended by him, and the colonel had to repeat the order, when the rope was cut by a single blow, and Brown fell through about five inches, his knees falling on a level with the position occupied by his feet before the rope was cut. With the fall his arms, below the elbows, flew up horizontally, his hands clinched; and his arms gradually fell, but by spasmodic motions. There was very little motion of his person for several moments, and soon the wind blew his lifeless body to and fro. His face, upon the scaffold, was turned a little east of south, and in front of him were the cadets, commanded by Major Gilman. My command was still in front of the cadets, all facing south. One howitzer I assigned to Mr. Trueheart on the left of the cadets, and with the other I remained on the right. Other troops occupied different positions around the scaffold, and altogether it was an imposing but very solemn scene. I was much impressed with the thought that he might in a few minutes receive the sentence, "Depart, ye wicked, into everlasting fire!" I hope that he was prepared to die, but I am doubtful. He refused to have a minister with him. His wife visited him last evening. His body was taken back to the jail, and at six o'clock P.M. was sent to his wife at Harper's Ferry. When it arrived, the coffin was opened, and his wife saw the remains, after which it was again opened at the depot before leaving for Baltimore, lest there should be an imposition. We leave for home via Richmond to-morrow.

In the summer of 1860, the Jacksons vacationed in historic Northampton, Massachusetts, home of the great eighteenth century theologian and pastor Jonathan Edwards. They took advantage of the hydropathic baths and the bracing New England climate. The physical benefits to Mrs. Jackson were so great that Major Jackson decided to leave her there for another month while he returned to his school duties in Lexington. Portions of two letters remain which reflect his interest in gardening and longing for her return. Their last prewar separation took place when she traveled to her sister Susan's wedding in North Carolina in February and remained through March 1861.

AUGUST, 1860 Little one, I must tell you what is in your garden. First and foremost, there is a very long row of celery; this is due to Hetty, and I told her that as she had succeeded so well I wouldn't touch its culture; though when it comes upon the table, and my little pet is here to enjoy it with me, I do not expect to be so chary of it.

You have also Lima beans, snap beans, carrots, parsnips, salsify, onions, cabbage, turnips, beets, potatoes, and some inferior muskmelons. Now, do you think you have enough vegetables? I am just thinking and thinking about that little somebody away up there.

SEPTEMBER 25, 1860 In answer to your question how you are to come, I should say, with your husband, if no other arrangement can be effected. If you don't meet with an opportunity of an escort to New York or farther, see if the doctor can't get you one to Springfield, upon the condition that you pay the expense. I don't want you to pass through Springfield alone, as you have to change cars there, and you might meet with some accident; but as visitors invite the doctor to make excursions with them, can't you invite him to make one with you to Springfield, and after he sees you on the right train, sit in the same car until you reach the depot in New York, where you may expect to find your *esposo* waiting for you? Be sure to write, and also telegraph, as I would rather go all the way to Round Hill than for you to come through Springfield alone. Your husband feels bright, and the light of his approaching little sunshine makes him still brighter. Whenever you write or telegraph for him, you may expect him to come for you in double-quick time.

FEBRUARY 18, 1861 My precious little darling, your husband has returned from the Institute, had his dinner all alone, and feels sad enough this afternoon; but I trust that my little pet has had a pleasant day's travel, and that the kind providence of God has kept her from all accident and danger, and has spread out before her many enjoyments. I hope that you will be greatly prospered during all your absence. The day here has been very changeable, alternating between sunshine and snow. I hope the Richmond weather is better, for I have been thinking you might be too much exposed in shopping. However, I hope you have taken a carriage, if necessary, and have taken good care of my little one.

FEBRUARY 19, 1861 My darling pet, your husband feels a loneliness for which he can hardly account, but he knows if his darling were here he wouldn't feel this. I have been busy, but still the feeling exists. I follow you in mind and heart, and think of you at the different points of your route.

FEBRUARY 23, 1861 I was very thankful to our kind Heavenly Father for his protecting care extended over my little pet, as stated in your letter. I do delight to receive letters from my little woman. If Sue is approachable on the Avery question, tell her she must be very litigious if she finds it necessary to engage the services of a member of the legal profession for life! Tell her we have them here from a mere tyro up to a judge of the Federal court, though do not mention the subject to her if you think it would be at all unpleasant. On Saturday I sent your boy, George, with your horse and wagon down to Thompson's landing, and brought up a barrel of nice Richmond sweet potatoes. I have laid aside the best, and hope they will keep till my little pet gets home. What think you? I went down to your henhouse yesterday evening, pursuant to orders, and, looking into the nests, found nine fresh eggs besides the Deaver [a porcelain egg bought of a man of that name], and, appropriating eight of them, I returned, leaving one in each nest.

FEBRUARY 27, 1861 This is a beautiful day here, and I have been thinking how blessful Sue's married life will be if her bridal day is its true emblem. . . . We had quite a treat last night in the performance of a company in Druidical costumes, making exquisite music upon instruments constructed of ox-horns, copied from the Druidical instruments in the British Museum.

MARCH 16, 1861 Amy has gone to grace the wedding of one of her colored friends by her imposing presence. George left for C——'s on the morning of March 1st, and I haven't seen his delectable face since. I am thankful to say that everything is working well at home. I expect to continue sending you letters as long as you stay away. You had better come home if you want to stop this correspondence. I have been working to-day at your garden fence to keep your chickens out, and also to prevent egress and ingress between our garden and that of Señor Deaver.

Your peas are just beginning to make their appearance above ground.... The colored Sabbath-school is greatly blessed in numbers and teachers, and is doing a good work.... Your friends here remember my darling with much interest.

Chapter Five

SECESSION AND WAR

The political turbulence of the times is not reflected in Jackson's letters to his wife, but his views are well-known by historians. Thomas Jackson was a Union man, a Democrat, and a firm believer in states rights. He disagreed with northern and southern radicals and opposed secession when Virginians were first called upon to join the new Confederacy of Southern States. The majority of his fellow citizens agreed in their opposition to breaking from the Union when the first vote was held on April 4, 1861. When President Abraham Lincoln called for every state to provide a quota of volunteers to "suppress the rebellion," Virginians, among them Stonewall Jackson, changed their sentiments overnight. By a vote of 88 to 55 the Old Dominion joined the Confederacy on April 17, and Governor Letcher called for volunteers to defend the state from invasion. Years later Anna Jackson remembered that her husband "deplored the collision most earnestly. He believed that patriotic statesmanship might have averted it. He loved the Union as only one who fought under the flag could love it. He would have died to have saved it in its purity and its just relations. But he believed that the constitutional rights of the States had been invaded, and he never had a doubt as to where his allegiance was due. His sword belonged to his State." In the assessment of Jackson's best biographer "the Confederacy as Jackson envisioned it [was] the next step in the history of Christian people. He would serve it and, by doing so, glorify God. To Jackson, this war was a call to wage both a political battle and a religious crusade . . . he would ride forward to do the Lord's work in the best way he could: as a soldier." [3]

The Institute looked to Jackson to lead the cadets to Richmond and to drill the recruits pouring into the improvised camps. On the trip to the state capitol, Jackson sent a quick letter to Anna. In not many days a commission as Colonel of Volunteers was put before the state convention. When asked who this major from VMI was, the delegate from Rockbridge County rose and replied, "He is a man who, if you order him to hold a post, will never leave it alive to be captured by the enemy." Colonel Jackson was ordered to Harpers Ferry to take command of Virginia troops.

APRIL 22, 1861   My little darling, the command left Staunton on a special train at about a quarter-past ten this morning. We are now stopping for a short time on the eastern slope of the Blue Ridge. The train will hardly reach Richmond before night. The war spirit here, as well as at other points of the line, is intense. The cars had scarcely

stopped before a request was made that I would leave a
cadet to drill a company.

APRIL 23, 1861, RICHMOND   The cadets are encamped
on the Fair grounds, which is about a mile and a half out
of the city, on the left side of the road. We have excellent
quarters. Colonel Robert E. Lee of the army is here, and
has been made major-general. This I regard as of more
value to us than to have General Scott as commander; as
it is understood that General Lee is to be our commander-
in-chief, and I regard him as a better officer than General
Scott. So far as we hear, God is crowning our cause with
success, but I don't wish to send rumors to you. I will try
to give facts as they become known, though I may not have
time to write more than a line or so. The governor and
others holding responsible offices have not enough time
for their duties, they are so enormous at this date.

APRIL 24, 1861, FAIR GROUNDS   I am unable to give
you the information I would like respecting things here.
The State troops are constantly arriving. The Fair grounds
are to be made the place for a school of practice. William
[Anna's brother, Major W.W. Morrison, who had held an
office under the United States government] passed through
to-day on his way home, and looks very well. He says there
is great uneasiness at Washington. His resignation was
accepted, although they desired him to remain. Major-

General Lee is commander-in-chief of all the land and naval forces in the State.

APRIL 25, 1861 The scene here, my darling pet, looks quite animated. Troops are continually arriving. Yesterday about seven hundred came in from South Carolina. . . . I received your precious letter, in which you speak of coming here in the event of my remaining. I would like very much to see my sweet little face, but my darling had better remain at her own home, as my continuance here is very uncertain.

APRIL 27, 1861, WINCHESTER, VIRGINIA I came from Richmond yesterday, and expect to leave here about half-past two o'clock this afternoon for Harper's Ferry. On last Saturday the Governor handed me my commission as Colonel of Virginia Volunteers, the post which I prefer above all others, and has given me an independent command. Little one, you must not expect to hear from me very often, as I expect to have more work than I have ever had in the same length of time before; but don't be concerned about your husband, for our kind Heavenly Father will give every needful aid.

APRIL 30 OR MAY 1, 1861 I am very much gratified with my command, and would rather have this post than any other in the State. I am in tolerable health, probably a little better than usual, if I had enough sleep. I haven't time now to do more than to tell you how much I love you.

MAY 3, 1861 I feel better this morning than I have for some time, having got more sleep than usual last night. Your precious letters have been reaching me from time to time, and gladden your husband's heart.

Colonel Jackson's five man staff included Major John Thomas Lewis Preston, a fellow professor at VMI and close friend, as "assistant adjutant general," and Major James W. Massie, also wearing the blue uniform of the Institute, as "inspector general." While Jackson ordered the continual drilling of the recruits by VMI cadets, the Virginia state government approved the Confederate Constitution and formally joined the new nation. The War Department of the Confederacy assigned the command of all the forces at Harper's Ferry to General Joseph Johnston, one of the most experienced and senior ranked officers of the nation.

Anna moved in with Mr. and Mrs. William N. Page after her husband's departure. In May, pursuant to his wishes, she closed up their Lexington home, sent the family servants to "good homes among the permanent residents," and moved back to Cottage Home in North Carolina.

MAY 8, 1861 At present I am living in an elegant mansion, with Major Preston in my room. Mr. Massie is on my staff, and left this morning for Richmond as bearer of dispatches, but will return in a few days. I am strengthening my position, and if attacked shall, with the blessing of Providence, repel the enemy. I am in good health, considering the great amount of labor which devolves upon me, and the loss of sleep to which I am subjected, but I hope to have a good sleep to-night, and trust that my habits will be more regular in the future. Colonels Preston and Massie have been of great service to me. Humanly speaking, I don't see how I could have accomplished the amount of work I have done without them. . . . Oh, how I would love to see your precious face!

MAY 27, 1861, HARPER'S FERRY My precious darling, I suppose you have heard that General Joseph E. Johnston, of the Confederate army, has been placed in command here. You must not concern yourself about the change. Colonel Preston will explain it all to you. I hope to have more time, as long as I am not in command of a post, to write longer letters to my darling pet.

MAY 30 OR JUNE 1, 1861 I am in command of the Virginia troops stationed here, and am doing well. I have been superseded by General Johnston, as stated in a former letter, but so far as I have yet learned, I have not been ordered to the Northwest . . .

I am very thankful to an ever-kind Providence for enabling you so satisfactorily to arrange our home matters. I just love my business little woman. Let Mr. Tebbs have the horse and rockaway at his own price; and if he is not able to pay for them, you may give them to him, as he is a minister of the Gospel. . . . I have written as you requested to Winchester, that if you were there, to come on; but, my little pet, whilst I should be delighted to see you, yet if you have not started, do not think of coming. . . . My habitual prayer is that our kind Heavenly Father will give unto my darling every needful blessing, and that she may have that "peace which passeth all understanding!"

JUNE 4, 1861, HARPER'S FERRY   Little one, you wrote me that you wanted longer letters, and now just prepare yourself to have your wish gratified. You say that your husband never writes you any news. I suppose you meant military news, for I have written you a great deal about your *esposo* and how much he loves you. What do you want with military news? Don't you know that it is unmilitary and unlike an officer to write news respecting one's post? You wouldn't wish your husband to do an unofficer-like thing, would you? I have a nice, green yard, and if you were only here, how much we could enjoy it together! But do not attempt to come, as before you could get here I might be ordered elsewhere. My chamber is on the second story, and the roses climb even to that height, and come into my window, so that I have to push them out, when I want to lower it. I wish you could see with me the beautiful roses in the yard and garden, and upon the wall of the house here; but my sweet, little sunny face is what I want to see most of all. Little one, you are so precious to somebody's heart! I have been greatly blessed by our kind Heavenly Father, in health and otherwise, since leaving home. The troops here have been divided into brigades, and the Virginia forces under General Johnston constitute the First Brigade, of which I am in command.

JUNE 14, 1861 We are about leaving this place. General Johnston has withdrawn his troops from the Heights (Maryland and Virginia), has blown up and burnt the railroad bridge across the Potomac, and is doing the same with respect to the public buildings. Yesterday morning, I was directed to get ready to evacuate the public buildings. Yesterday morning, I was directed to get ready to evacuate the place, and in the evening expected to march, but up to the present time the order has not come. I am looking for it at any moment, and, as I am at leisure, will devote myself to writing to my precious pet. I am very thankful to our kind Heavenly Father for having sent Joseph [Anna's brother] for you, and I trust that you are now safely and happily at Cottage Home, and that you found the family all well. You speak of others knowing more about me than my darling does, and say you have heard through others that I am a brigadier-general. By this time I suppose you have found out that the report owes its origin to Madam Rumor.

JUNE 18, 1861 On Sunday, by order of General Johnston, the entire force left Harper's Ferry, marched towards

Winchester, passed through Charlestown, and halted for
the night about two miles this side. The next morning we
moved towards the enemy, who were between Martinsburg
and Williamsport, Maryland, and encamped for the
night at Bunker Hill. Yesterday morning we were to have
marched at sunrise, and I hoped that in the evening, or this
morning, we should have engaged the enemy; but, instead
of doing so, General Johnston made some disposition for
receiving the enemy if they should attack us, and thus we
were kept until about noon, when he gave the order to
return towards Winchester. Near sunset we reached this
place, which is about three miles north of Winchester, on
the turnpike leading thence to Martinsburg. On Sunday,
when our troops were marching on the enemy, they were so
inspirited as apparently to forget the fatigue of the march;
and though some of them were suffering from hunger,
this and other privations appeared to be forgotten, and
the march continued at the rate of about three miles an
hour. But when they were ordered to retire, their reluctance
was manifested by their snail-like pace. I hope the general
will do something soon. Since we left Harper's Ferry, an
active movement towards repelling the enemy is, of course,
expected. I trust that through the blessing of God we shall
soon be given an opportunity of driving the invaders from
this region.

Colonel Jackson now commanded only the 1st Virginia
Brigade composed of four infantry regiments—the 2nd

under VMI graduate Colonel James W. Allen, the 4th under Winchester attorney Lt. Colonel Lewis T. Moore, the 5th led by sixty-year-old Colonel Kenton Harper, and the 27th directed by Harvard Law School graduate John Echols. Two new staff members were added to Colonel Jackson's military family: Edwin Lee as aide and Sandy Pendleton, son of the former Episcopal pastor of the Lexington church, now an artillery commander in the army, as acting adjutant general. One of the most valuable members of Jackson's entourage was his personal servant Jim, who remained faithfully by his side to the end.

JUNE 22, 1861, HEADQUARTERS FIRST VIRGINIA BRIGADE, CAMP STEPHEN My darling *esposita*, I am at present about four miles north of Martinsburg, and on the road leading to Williamsport, Maryland. General Johnston ordered me to Martinsburg on last Wednesday, and there appeared to be a prospect for a battle on Thursday, but the enemy withdrew from our side of the river. Our troops are very anxious for an engagement, but this is the second time the enemy have retreated before our advance. However, we may have an engagement any day. Rumor reports the Federal troops as concentrating near Shepherdstown, on the Maryland side of the Potomac. A great number of families have left their homes. By order of General Johnston I have destroyed a large number of locomotives and cars on the Baltimore and Ohio Railroad. ... I have just learned that the enemy are again crossing into Virginia at Williamsport, and I am making the necessary arrangements for advancing to meet them.

JUNE 24, 1861   I advanced with Colonel J.W. Allen's regiment and Captain Pendleton's Battery, but the enemy retreated across the river, and, after reconnoitering their camp, I returned to my present position, four miles north of Martinsburg. The Federal troops were in two camps, one estimated at about six hundred, and the other at nine hundred. You spoke of the cause of the South being gloomy. It is not so here. I am well satisfied that the enemy are afraid to meet us, and our troops are anxious for an engagement. A few days since Colonel A.P. Hill, who had been sent to Romney, dispatched a detachment to burn a bridge eighteen miles west of Cumberland. The enterprise was successful. The enemy lost two guns and their colors. I regret to see our ladies making those things they call "Havelocks" [a covering to protect the head and neck from the sun], as their time and money could be much more usefully employed in providing haversacks for the soldiers, many of whom have none in which to carry their rations. I have been presented with three Havelocks, but I do not intend to wear them, for, as far as I am concerned, I shall show that such protection is unnecessary in this climate.

JUNE 28, 1861, BERKELEY COUNTY   I am bivouacking. I sleep out of doors without any cover except my bedding, but have not felt any inconvenience from it that I am aware of in the way of impaired health. Last evening, opposite Williamsport, one of our men was shot in the abdomen by the enemy, but he is still living, and I trust will recover. I am inclined to think it was done by a Virginian rather than a Northerner. There is a great deal of disloyalty in this county, although it has diminished. Mr. Edwin Lee, son-in-law of General Pendleton, is my aid, and Sandy Pendleton is my ordnance officer and acting adjutant-general. Last night the news came, after I had retired, that the enemy had packed their wagons with baggage, thus indicating a move in some direction. I didn't trouble my command, but merely gave such orders as were necessary to prevent their approach without giving me timely notice; but, in consequence, I had my rest disturbed, and am feeling the effects of it to-day. Yesterday Lieutenant Bowman, of the Eighth Regiment, Pennsylvania Volunteers, who was captured some time since opposite Williamsport by Colonel J.E.B. Stuart, of the cavalry, and now in Richmond on his parole of honor, sent a letter via here to Williamsport which required us to send a flag of truce. All went off well.

JULY 4, 1861, DARKESVILLE My precious darling, day before yesterday I learned that the enemy had crossed the Potomac and were advancing upon me. I immediately ordered my command under arms, and gave such instructions as I desired to have carried out until I should be heard from again, and with Captain Pendleton's Battery and one regiment of Virginia volunteers advanced to meet the

Federal troops. After proceeding to the locality which had been indicated as occupied by them, and ascertaining the position of their advance, I made the necessary movement for bringing a small part of my force into action. Soon the firing commenced, and the advance of the enemy was driven back. They again advanced and were repulsed. My men got possession of a house and barn, which gave them a covered position and an effective fire; but finding that the enemy were endeavoring to get in my rear and that my men were being endangered, I gave the order to their colonel that, if pressed, he must fall back. He obeyed, and fell back. The artillery of the foe opened upon me, and I directed Captain Pendleton to take a favorable position in rear and return their fire with one gun. His first ball cleared the road, which was occupied by the enemy. [It is said that, before firing this first ball upon the enemy, the reverend officer lifted his eyes to heaven and uttered the prayer, "Lord, have mercy upon their souls!"] I still continued to fall back, checking the enemy when it became necessary, so as to give time for my baggage to get into column at camp before I should arrive there, as one of my objects in advancing was to keep the enemy from reaching my camp before my wagons could get out of the way. Besides my cavalry, I had only one regiment engaged, and one cannon, though I had ordered up two other regiments, so as to use them if necessary. My cannon fired only eight times, while the enemy fired about thirty-five times; but the first fire of Captain Pendleton's Battery was probably worth more than all of theirs. I desired, as far as practicable, to save my ammunition. My orders from General Johnston required me to retreat in the event of the advance in force of the enemy, so as soon as I ascertained that he was in force I obeyed my instructions. I had twelve wounded and thirteen killed and missing. My cavalry took forty-nine prisoners. A number of the enemy were killed, but I do not know how many. As I obeyed my orders, and fell back, after ascertaining that the Federals were in force, the killed of the enemy did not fall into our hands. My officers and men behaved beautifully, and were anxious for a battle, this being only a skirmish. [The affair was known as that of "Falling Waters."] I wrote out my official report last night, and think General Johnston forwarded it to Richmond. This morning one of his staff-officers told me that the general had recommended me for a brigadier-general. I am very thankful that an ever-kind Providence made me an instrument in carrying out General Johnston's orders so successfully. . . . The enemy are celebrating the 4th of July in Martinsburg, but we are not observing the day.

After the skirmish at Falling Waters, General Johnston ordered the army to fall back to Winchester, a city destined to fall into the hands of the enemy and be retaken many times throughout the war. On July 8, Colonel Jackson received a short message from Robert E. Lee announcing Jackson's promotion to brigadier general.

JULY 1861 I have been officially informed of my promotion to be a brigadier-general of the Provisional Army of the Southern Confederacy, but it was prior to my skirmish with the enemy. My letter from the Secretary of War was dated 17th of June. Thinking it would be gratifying to you, I send the letters of Generals Lee and Johnston. From the latter you will see that he desired my promotion for my conduct on the 2nd and 3rd instant. On the 3rd I did nothing more than join General Johnston. My promotion was beyond what I anticipated, as I only expected it to be in the volunteer forces of the State. One of my greatest desires for advancement is the gratification it will give my darling, and [the opportunity] of serving my country more efficiently. I have had all that I ought to desire in the line of promotion. I should be very ungrateful if I were not contented, and exceedingly thankful to our kind Heavenly Father. May his blessing ever rest on you is my fervent prayer. Try to live near to Jesus, and secure that peace which flows like a river.

JULY 1861, WINCHESTER It was your husband that did so much mischief at Martinsburg. To destroy so many fine locomotives, cars, and railroad property was a sad work, but I had my orders, and my duty was to obey. If the cost of the property could only have been expended in disseminating the gospel of the Prince of Peace, how much good might have been expected! . . . You must not be concerned at our falling back to this place [Winchester]. . . .

One of the most trying things here is the loss of sleep. Last night I was awakened by a messenger from the house of a friend where some cavalry had stopped. One of his fair daughters took it into her head that the cavalry belonged to the enemy, whereupon she wrote me a note, much to my discomfort; but the field-officer of the day went over to examine into the case, and found the officer in command was one of his friends. The people here are very kind; so much so that I have to decline many invitations to accept their hospitalities. At present I am in a very comfortable building, but we are destitute of furniture, except such things as we have been able to gather together. I am very thankful to our Heavenly Father for having given me such a fine brigade.

JULY 16, 1861, WINCHESTER Last evening the enemy encamped at Bunker Hill, about ten miles from us, and this morning we would have given them a warm reception had they advanced, but we have heard nothing respecting their movements to-day. The news from the Northwest is unfavorable, as you have probably seen in the papers, but we must not be discouraged. God will, I am well satisfied, in His own good time and way, give us the victory. . . . In reply to your queries, I am sleeping on the floor of a good room, but I have been sleeping out in camp several weeks, and generally found that it agreed with me well, except when it rained, and even then it was but slightly objectionable. I find that sleeping in the open air, with no covering but my blankets and the blue sky for a canopy, is more refreshing than sleeping in a room. My table is rather poor, but usually I get corn-bread. All things considered, however, I am doing well. . . . As to writing so as to mail letters which would travel on Sunday, when it can be avoided, I have never had occasion, after years of experience, to regret our system. Although sister I—— gets letters from her husband every day, is she any happier than my *esposita*? Look how our kind Heavenly Father has prospered us! I feel well assured that in following our rule, which is Biblical, I am in the path of duty, and that no evil can come nigh me. All things work together for my good. But when my sweet one writes, let the letters be long, and your *esposo* hopes to send you full ones in return; and when the wars and troubles are all over, I trust that, through divine mercy, we shall have many happy days together.

While Jackson trained his men under the command of Joseph Johnston near Winchester, the strategic defense of Richmond lay twenty-five miles south of Washington, D.C. near Manassas Junction. There the 22,000 man Confederate Army under Pierre G.T. Beauregard prepared for the invasion that all knew would be coming soon. On July 18, General Beauregard sent the message to Johnston that Union General Irvin McDowell was heading his way with Federal forces numbering about 35,000 men. Johnston's 11,000 men slipped away from the not very vigilant Union General Robert

Patterson, who was supposed to hold them in place, and marched east to reinforce the troops at Manassas.

The first major battle of the war took place between armies of amateur soldiers, most of them teenage farmers. The engagement has become a byword for confusion, ineptitude, and unprecedented violence. When Jackson's troops arrived, they marched to the sound of the guns and went into position behind the Henry House near the straining and breaking Confederate left flank.

Thomas Jackson's defining moment in history had come. General Bernard Bee, a West Point classmate of Jackson's, rode to him and reported the collapse of his line. Jackson replied, "Sir, we will give them the bayonet!" Riding back into the middle of his fleeing men, Bee called out, "Look, men, there is Jackson standing like a stone wall. Let us determine to die here, and we will conquer!"

After some action on the Brigade's left, the opposing Yankee forces, with twice the number of men, made a blunt frontal assault on Jackson's line. He ordered his men and artillery to hold their fire till the enemy came within fifty yards. The blast of fire from Jackson's line sent the foe reeling backward. Twice more they came on and were mowed down. Then the newly christened Stonewall Jackson gave the order to charge and "yell like furies." The five Virginia regiments leaped forward and, with Confederate reinforcements coming on the field, drove the enemy from the field and back to Washington in confusion. The battle had hung in the balance. Both sides had fought with determination, but Jackson's timely defense and attack turned the tide.

DATE UNKNOWN 1861, MANASSAS   On the 18th of July I struck my tents, rolled them up, and left them on the ground, and about noon marched through Winchester, as I had been encamped on the other side of the town. About an hour and a half after leaving, I had the following order from General Johnston published to my brigade:

> Our gallant army under General Beauregard is now attacked by overwhelming numbers. The commanding general hopes that his troops will step out like men, and make a forced march to save the country.

At this stirring appeal the soldiers rent the air with shouts of joy, and all was eagerness and animation where before there had been only lagging and uninterested obedience. We continued our march until we reached Millwood, in Clarke County, where we halted for an hour or so, having found an abundance of good water, and there we took lunch. Resuming the march, my brigade continuing in front, we arrived at the Shenandoah River about dark. The water was waist-deep, but the men gallantly waded the river. This halting and crossing delayed us for some time; but about two o'clock in the morning we arrived at the little village of Paris, where we remained sleeping until nearly dawn. I mean the troops slept, as my men were so exhausted that I let them sleep while I kept watch myself. Bright and early we resumed the march, and the head of our column arrived at Piedmont, on the Manassas Gap Railroad, about six o'clock in the morning. After getting our breakfast, the brigade commenced going aboard of the cars, and the same day all that could be carried arrived at Manassas about four o'clock in the afternoon, without much suffering to my men or to myself. The next day we rested, and the following day was the memorable 21st of July.

JULY 22, 1861, MANASSAS   My precious Pet, yesterday we fought a great battle and gained a great victory, for which all the glory is due to *God alone*. Although under a heavy fire for several continuous hours, I received only one wound, the breaking of the longest finger of my left hand; but the doctor says the finger can be saved. It was broken about midway between the hand and knuckle, the ball passing on the side next the forefinger. Had it struck the center, I should have lost the finger. My horse was wounded, but not killed. Your coat got an ugly wound near the hip, but my servant, who is very handy, has so far repaired it that it doesn't show very much. My preservation was entirely due, as was the glorious victory, to our God, to who be all the honor, praise, and glory. The battle was the hardest that I have ever been in, but not near so hot in its fire. I commanded in the center more particularly, though one of my regiments extended to the right for some distance. There were other commanders on my right and left. Whilst great credit is due to other parts of our gallant army, God made my brigade more instrumental than any other in repulsing the main attack. This is for your information only; say nothing about it. Let others speak praise, not myself.

JULY 24, 1861   Mr. James Davidson's son, Frederick, and William Page (son of my dear friend) were killed. Young Riley's life was saved by his Bible, which was in the breast-pocket of his coat. . . . My finger troubles me considerably, and renders it very difficult for me to write, as the wind blows my paper, and I can only use my right hand. I have an excellent camping-ground about eight miles from Manassas on the road to Fairfax Court House. I am sleeping in a tent, and have requested that the one which my darling had the loving kindness to order for me should not be sent. If it is already made, we can use it in time of peace. . . . General Lee has recently gone to the western part of our State, and I hope we may soon hear that our God has again crowned our arms with victory.

The Battle of First Manassas was only the beginning of long casualty lists, with students, friends, and acquaintances of the Jacksons included among the wounded and slain. Because of increased command responsibilities, Stonewall Jackson added several more men to his staff. Major John H. Harmon became Jackson's quartermaster. Large, loud, incredibly profane, and unafraid of any man, he succeeded as few other quartermasters ever could. With thirteen children at home to feed, Jackson's army was just so many more hungry teenagers. Captain Wells J. Hawks, a native of Massachusetts and three term member of the Virginia legislature, managed Jackson's commissary department. As one historian has rightly observed, "Jackson handpicked men who possessed high moral character, strict punctuality, and exactitude to duty." [4]

The opposing armies settled into wary defensive positions and, as the weeks turned into months with no further movement, the more aggressive leaders like Stonewall Jackson became frustrated with the inactivity. Anna continued to plead with Thomas to take a furlough, but his sense of duty did not allow such luxury for himself or his men, including the officers.

Regimental band concerts were one of the pleasurable interludes of camp life, and General Jackson greatly enjoyed listening. His wife noted, however, that his talent for music was almost nonexistent, and he had her sing "Dixie" to him over and over again after he was informed that it was the most popular national tune.

AUGUST 5, 1861   And so you think the papers ought say more about your husband! My brigade is not a brigade of newspaper correspondents. I know that the First Brigade was the first to meet and pass our retreating forces—to push on with no other aid than the smiles of God; to boldly take its position with the artillery that was under my command—

to arrest the victorious foe in his onward progress—to hold him in check until reinforcements arrived—and finally to charge bayonets, and, thus advancing, pierce the enemy's center. I am well satisfied with what it did, and so are my generals, Johnston and Beauregard. It is not to be expected that I should receive the credit that Generals Beauregard and Johnston would, because I was under them; but I am thankful to my ever-kind Heavenly Father that He makes me content to await His own good time and pleasure for commendation—knowing that all things work together for my good. If my brigade can always play so important and useful a part as it did in the last battle, I trust I shall ever be most grateful. As you think your papers do not notice me enough, I send a specimen, which you will see from the upper part of the paper is a leader. My darling, never distrust our God, who doeth all things well. In due time He will make manifest all His pleasure, which is all His people should desire. You must not be concerned at seeing other parts of the army lauded, and my brigade not mentioned. "Truth is mighty and will prevail." When the official reports are published, if not before, I expect to see justice done this noble body of patriots. My command consists of the Second, Fourth, Fifth, Twenty-seventh, and Thirty-third regiments of Virginia Volunteers, commanded respectively by Colonels James W. Allen, James F. Preston, Kenton Harper, W.W. Gordon, and A.C. Cummings; and, in addition, we have Colonel Pendleton's Battery. My staff-officers are Lieutenant Colonel Francis B. Jones, acting adjutant-general; Lieutenant Colonel J.W. Massie, aide; Lieutenant A.S. Pendleton, ordnance officer; Captain John A. Harman, quartermaster; and Captain W.J. Hawkes, commissary.

AUGUST 1861 I have received a circular to the effect that two professors must return to the Institute at the opening of the session, the 1st of September, and that if that number do not consent to return, the Board of Visitors will designate two; and if they decline, their seats will thereby be declared vacant, and the board would fill them. I declined returning. How would you like going back to Lexington in September, and staying there for the remainder of the war? ... I am glad that the battle [First Manassas] was fought on your birthday, so you can never tell me any more that I forget your birthday. See if I don't always remember it, though I do not my own. If General Lee remains in the Northwest, I would like to go there and give my feeble aid, as an humble instrument in the hand of Providence in retrieving the downtrodden loyalty of that part of my native State. But I desire to be wherever those over me may decide, and I am content here. The success of our cause is the earthly object near my heart; and, if I know myself, all I am and have is at the service of my country.

AUGUST 17, 1861 You want to know whether I could get a furlough. My darling, I can't be absent from my command, as my attention is necessary in preparing my troops for hard fighting should it be required; and as my; officers and soldiers are not permitted to go and see their wives and families, I ought not to see my *esposita*, as it might make the troops feel that they were badly treated, and that I consult my own pleasure and comfort regardless of theirs: so you had better stay at Cottage Home for the present, as I do not know how long I shall remain here.

AUGUST 22, 1861 Don't you wish your *esposo* would get sick, and have to get a sick leave and go home, so that you couldn't envy sister Sue? Sickness may compel me for a time to retire from camp, but, through the blessing of God, I have been able to continue in command of my brigade. . . . Still much remains undone that I desire to see effected. But in a short time I hope to be more instrumental in serving my country. Every officer and soldier who is able to do duty ought to be busily engaged in military preparation by hard drilling, in order that, through the blessing of God, we may be victorious in the battles which in His all-wise providence may await us. I wish my darling could be with me now and enjoy the sweet music of the brass band of the Fifth Regiment. It is an excellent band.

Don't put any faith in the assertion that there will be no more fighting till October. It may not be till then; and God grant that, if consistent with His will, it may never be. Surely, I desire no more, if our country's independence can be secured without it. As I said before leaving my darling, so say I now, that if I fight for my country, it is from a sense of duty—a hope that through the blessing of Providence I may be enabled to serve her, and not merely because I prefer the strife of battle to the peaceful enjoyments of home. . . . Yesterday the enemy drove in our pickets, and General Longstreet sent me a request to move forward with my brigade, and the consequence was that after advancing beyond Fairfax Court House six miles it turned out that the enemy did not intend to attack, and I had a ride of twelve miles for nothing; and my wounded finger suffered from it, but I trust, with the blessing of an ever-kind Providence, it will soon be well. I meet with a number of old army friends and some of my classmates, which is quite a pleasure. The country about Fairfax Court House is beautiful. As I came in sight of the place, the sun was near setting, and with its mellowed light greatly contributed to beautify the scenery. I am writing under a Sibley tent, which is of a conical form, so constructed as to allow fire to be used, having an opening at the top for the escape of smoke; though as yet I have had my fires in the house. The weather is quite cool at night. What do you think? This morning I had a kind of longing to see our lot—not our house, for I did not want to enter its desolate chambers, as it would be too sad not to find my little sunshine there.

AUGUST OR SEPTEMBER 1861, CAMP HARMAN, NEAR MANASSAS Yesterday I received two letters from one little jewel of mine at Cottage Home, and I am just going to read them over and over again and answer.

First, in reference to coming to see your *esposo*, what would you do for privacy in camp? I tell you there are more inconveniences attending camp life for a lady than little pet is aware of; and worst of all is the danger you might encounter in such a trip, as the cars are so crowded with soldiers. But I would dearly love to have my darling here at this time, and think I might probably be able to get a room for you with a kind family in whose yard I have my tent. The family is exceedingly obliging, and we could have delightful times together, as I have to stay about quarters on account of my wounded finger. However, through the blessing of an ever-kind Providence, it is now much improved. Should there be a good escort coming on and returning, little one can come; but you must not spare any expense in making your trip comfortable. You must hire a carriage whenever you haven't a safe and good conveyance, in the event of your coming. Last Sabbath Dr. Pendleton preached at my headquarters in the morning, and Rev. Peyton Harrison preached in the evening. . . . If the war is carried on with vigor, I think that, under the blessing of God, it will not last long, though we may frequently have little local troubles along the frontier. . . . At present it would be improper for me to be absent from my brigade a single day, but just as soon as duty will permit I hope to see my sunshiny face. The reason of my changing my advice about your coming was probably in consequence of orders respecting a march. Within the last three weeks I have had to march off several times, but in each case I have been privileged to return to

my present encampment, where I desire to stay as long as
I am to remain inactive, for it is the best encampment I
have had. We are blessed with excellent water and a good
drill-ground. Little one can come on with the first good
opportunity, if she is willing to bear the unexpected
occurrences of war. I know not one day what will take place
the next, but I do know that I am your doting *esposo*.

General Jackson consented to Anna's traveling to Northern
Virginia to visit him and she arrived on September 9. They
had been apart for five months and her visit brought great
happiness to both of them. He took her through the beautiful
Fairfax countryside and to the bloody battlefield of Manassas.
She loved to see his pride for the Stonewall Brigade encamped
nearby and was thrilled by the review of General Johnston's
entire command. She remarked years later that camp life held
a very real charm for her, and she would not have willingly
left her husband. When orders came to move the camp, she
sorrowfully returned to North Carolina.

The only military activity in Virginia at that time was an
ineffectual and bumbling expedition into the mountains of the
western part of the state by another Confederate army, which
added nothing to the reputation of Robert E. Lee and wrecked
the budding careers of several other Confederate generals.

Joseph Johnston's army was destined to remain in the
lines in northern Virginia until spring, suffering many
casualties from disease. Unlike many other commanders,
Jackson continued drill and strict discipline to keep his men

ready for combat and help stave off boredom and restlessness. Ever interested in the spiritual welfare of his men and his own growth in grace, Stonewall Jackson promoted regular preaching to his men and supported the regimental chaplains in every way possible. His appreciation for the Rev. Dr. Robert Lewis Dabney and his preaching would eventually result in Dabney's promotion to adjutant general on Jackson's staff. On October 7, Stonewall Jackson was promoted to major general by the Confederate Congress.

SEPTEMBER 24, 1861   I am going to write a letter to my darling pet *esposita*, who paid me such a sweet visit, and whose dear face I can still see, though she is way down in the Old North State. If my darling were here, I know she would enjoy General Jones's band, which plays very sweetly. We are still at the same encampment as when you left, and I have the promise of three more wall tents. Yesterday Rev. Dr. William Brown visited Munson's Hill, and took a peep at the Yankees.... The Board of Visitors of the Institute met in Richmond, and decided if the professors did not return they would fill their places, superintendents and all. Suppose they ask you to go back. Are you going to do so, or will you let them fill your chair? Colonel Echols returned this morning, but does not bring, to our finite minds, very good news. General Floyd was only about thirty miles west of Lewisburg, and General Wise was fifteen miles in advance of him. General Lee, with four regiments, had gone on to General Wise.

SEPTEMBER 1861   Monday morning. This is a beautiful and lovely morning—beautiful emblem of the morning of eternity in heaven. I greatly enjoy it after our cold, chilly weather, which has made me feel doubtful of my capacity, humanly speaking, to endure the campaign, should we remain long in tents. But God, our God, does, and will do, all things well; and if it is His pleasure that I should remain in the field, He will give me the ability to endure all its fatigues. I hope my little sunshiny face is as bright as this lovely day. Yesterday I heard a good sermon from the chaplain of the Second Regiment, and at night I went over to Colonel Garland's regiment of Longstreet's Brigade, and heard an excellent sermon from the Rev. Mr. Granberry, of the Methodist church, of whom you may have heard me speak in times past.

SEPTEMBER 26, 1861   I did not have room enough in my last letter, nor have I time this morning, to write as much as I desired about Dr. Dabney's sermon yesterday. His text was from Acts, seventh chapter and fifth verse. He stated that the word God being in italics indicated that it was not in the original, and he thought it would have been better not to have been in the translation. It would then have read: "Calling upon and saying, Lord Jesus, receive my spirit." He spoke of Stephen, the first martyr under the new dispensation, like Abel, the first under the old, dying by the hand of violence, and then drew a graphic picture of his probably broken limbs, mangled flesh and features, conspiring to heighten his agonizing suffering. But in the midst of this intense pain, God, in His infinite wisdom and mercy, permitted him to see the heavens opened, so that he might behold the glory of God, and Jesus, of whom he was speaking, standing on the right hand of God. Was not such a heavenly vision enough to make him forgetful of his sufferings? He beautifully and forcibly described the death of the righteous, and as forcibly that of the wicked. . . .

Strangers as well as Lexington friends are very kind to me. I think about eight days since a gentleman sent me a half-barrel of tomatoes, bread, etc., and I received a letter, I am inclined to think from the same, desiring directions how to send a second supply. I received from Colonel Ruff a box of beautifully packed and delicately flavored plums; also a bottle of blackberry vinegar from Misses B——. What I need is a more grateful heart to the "Giver of every good and perfect gift."

OCTOBER 1, 1861, CAMP NEAR FAIRFAX COURT-HOUSE Yesterday I rode on to the station, and while there President Davis, very unexpectedly to me, arrived in a single car; the remaining part of the train, I suppose, stopped at the Junction to unload. He looked quite thin. His reception was hearty cheer from the troops. He took his seat in an ambulance-like carriage, and as he passed on his way to the Court-House the air rang with the soldiers' welcoming cheers. He was soon met by a troop of horses, and a horse for himself. Leaving his carriage and mounting his horse, he proceeded on his way, escorted by the cavalry, about four thousand of the First Corps (General Beauregard). The troops belonged to Generals Longstreet, D.R. Jones, and Philip St. George Cocke. It was quite an imposing pageant. . . .

Yesterday I saw President Davis review. He took up his quarters with General Beauregard, where, in company with Colonels Preston, Harmon, and Echols, I called upon him this morning at about half-past ten o'clock. He looks thin, but does not seem to be as feeble as yesterday. His voice and manners are very mild. I saw no exhibition of that fire which I had supposed him to possess. The President introduced the subject of the condition of my section of the State, but did not even so much as intimate that he designed sending me there. I told him, when he spoke of my native region, that I felt a very deep interest in it. He spoke hopefully of that section, and highly of General Lee.

OCTOBER 14, 1861   I am going to write a letter to the very sweetest little woman I know, the only sweetheart I have; can you guess who she is? I tell you, I would like to see my sunshine, even this brightest of days. My finger has been healed over for some time, and I am blest by an ever-kind Providence with the use of it, though it is still partially stiff. I hope, however, in the course of time, that I shall be again blest with its perfect use. . . .

If I get into winter-quarters, will little ex-Anna Morrison come and keep house for me, and stay with me till the opening of the campaign of 1862? Now, remember, I don't want to change housekeepers. I want the same one all the time. I am very thankful to that God who withholds no good thing from me (though I am so utterly unworthy and ungrateful) for making me a major-general in the Provisional Army of the Confederate States. The commission dates from the 7th of October.

OCTOBER 21, 1861, CENTREVILLE For several days your *esposo* has been here, and has an extra nice room, the parlor of a Mr. Grigsby, who has promised that he will also let me have another room for my chamber, and then I can use the parlor for my office. He has very kindly offered me the use of his library. The walls of his parlor are hung with pictures and paintings, including large portraits on opposite sides, I suppose of the *exposo* and *esposa*. The carpet has been removed, but an abundance of seats have been left, two settees among them. Mr. Grigsby is apparently a man of much character, and I am very much pleased with him. His wife is delicate, and two of his sons have typhoid fever, but are past the critical stage of the disease. He has not yet consented to my staff moving into the house, probably for fear of disturbing the sick. Colonel Jones has resigned and gone home, and Mr. Marshall went with him. They are both nice gentlemen.

OCTOBER 22, 1861, CENTREVILLE I am going to tell you just where your *esposo* is living for the present. Starting from Mr. Utterbach's on the Warrenton road towards the battleground of Manassas, a street turns off to the right from the Warrenton road. Following the street about one hundred yards brings you to a large stone house, with four chimneys, on the right-hand side of the road. Passing up a flight of steps of nearly eight feet brings you into the porch, after crossing which you enter a hall about ten feet wide, and you have only to come into the first door on your right if you wish to see your husband, seated on the left of a hickory fire, on the opposite side of the room, writing to his sweetheart, or to his *esposita*, whichever you may choose to call her. Looking around the room, you will see upon the mantel a statuette of a mother with a child in her arms, an oil painting of a beautiful boy, a globe lamp, two candelabra, and two vases. Above the mantel are two rose pictures. On either side of the fireplace is a window, and on the left of the fire are a pair of bellows and a large shovel. On the right are a pair of tongs, and a handsome feather broom for your *esposo* to sweep the hearth with. So far I have described only the southern wall. Turning your eyes to the right, you will see two windows on the western wall, looking towards the battle-ground of the 21st July. On the left end of this wall hangs the celebrated oil painting, "Beatrice Cenci." Between the windows is a large portrait (as I suppose) of Mrs. Grigsby. On the right of the right-hand window is a landscape painting. Upon the northern wall to the left of the door is a picture, "The Evening Prayer," with the invocation, "Defend us from all perils and dangers of the night." Near this hangs a thermometer. On the right of the door are two other works of art, and between them is a the library desk, which is kindly placed at my disposal. Upon the eastern wall, left end, is a picture of "Holyrood." Near it, but on the right, is a large portrait of Mr. Grigsby. About the center of the wall is a large mirror—on its right is a picture called "Innocence"—and *here* is your loving husband!

... Our success at Leesburg reflected credit upon Colonel Evans and his heroic brigade.

... I have written to Colonel Preston, of Lexington, to join me. My desire is to get a staff specially qualified for their duties, and that will render the greatest possible amount of service to their country. Last night, Drs. White [his pastor] and McFarland reached here and are staying with me. They are just from Synod at Petersburg, and give a very gratifying account of things there. Dr. McFarland is a noble specimen of character.

On October 28, orders came sending General Jackson to the Shenandoah Valley to take command of the militia gathered near Winchester and create a force that could contend with any possible Yankee encroachments. His emotional farewell to his old Brigade was delivered from the back of his horse, Little Sorrel, and was remembered by several soldiers in the ranks:

You are the brigade which turned the tide of battle on Manassas Plains and there gained for yourself imperishable honor, and your names will be handed down with honor attached in future history. You were the First Brigade in the Army of the Shenandoah, the First Brigade in the Army of the Potomac, the First Brigade in the Second Corps, and are the First Brigade in the hearts of your generals. I hope that you will be the First Brigade in this, our second struggle for independence, and in the future, on the fields on which the Stonewall Brigade are engaged, I expect to hear of crowning deeds of valor and of victories gloriously achieved! May God bless you all, Farewell! [5]

A letter to a newspaper by an Augusta County soldier in the Stonewall Brigade reveals the attitude of many of the men serving under his command: "Wherever the voice of our brave and beloved general is heard, we are ready to follow. I have read of the devotion of soldiers to their commanders, but history contains no parallel case of devotion and affection equal to that of the Stonewall Brigade for Major General Jackson. We do not look upon him merely as our commander—do not regard him as a severe disciplinarian, as a politician, as a man seeking popularity—but as a Christian; brave man who appreciates the condition of a common soldier; as a fatherly protector; as one who endures all hardships in common with his followers; who never commands others to face danger without putting himself in the van. The confidence and esteem of the soldiers are always made known in exulting shouts whenever he makes his appearance." With such men, Stonewall Jackson was going to astound the world in the spring of 1862.

November 4, 1861 This morning I received orders to proceed to Winchester. I am assigned to the command of military district of the Northern frontier, between the Blue Ridge and the Alleghany Mountains, and I hope to have my little dove with me this winter. How do you like the programme? I trust I may be able to send for you after I get settled. I don't expect much sleep to-night, as my desire is to travel all night, if necessary, for the purpose of reaching Winchester before day to-morrow. My trust is in God for the defense of that country [the Valley]. I shall have great labor to perform, but, through the blessing of our ever-kind Heavenly Father, I trust that He will enable me to accomplish it. Colonel Preston and Sandy Pendleton go with me.

November 9, 1861 I trust that my darling little wife feels more gratitude to our kind Heavenly Father than pride or elation at my promotion. Continue to pray for me, that I may live to glorify God more and more, by serving Him and our country. . . . If you were only here, you would have a very nice house, the description of which I will postpone until after answering your letters; and if there isn't room, it will be deferred for the next letter, as it will take nearly a whole letter to tell you how very nice it is. And if your husband stays here this winter, he hopes to send one of his aides for one little somebody. You know very well who I mean by "little somebody."

And now for an answer to your questions; and without stating your questions, I will answer them. My command is enlarged, and embraces the Valley District, and the troops of this district constitute the Army of the Valley; but my command is not altogether independent, as it is embraced in the Department of Northern Virginia, of which General Johnston has the command. There are three armies in this department—one under General Beauregard, another under General Holmes, and the third under my command. My headquarters are for the present at Winchester. A major-general's rank is inferior to that of a full general. The rank of major-general does not appear to be recognized by the laws of the Confederate States, so far as I have seen; but there may be some law embraced in the Army Regulations which I have not seen. At all events, the President appoints them in the Provisional Army of the Confederate States, and these appointments are only for the war. As the regulations of the Army of the Confederate States do not require the rank of major-general, there is no pay and no staff appointed for it; but I expect to have two aides, and at least an adjutant-general. I am making up my staff slowly, in consequence of desiring to secure a good one, and some of them being at a distance. My promotion places me between a brigadier and a full general; but I don't think that either a major-general or a full general will be paid any more than $301 per month (the pay of a brigadier), but as commander of an army my additional pay is $100, making in all $401 per month. I send you a check for $1000, which I wish invested in Confederate bonds, as I think, as far as possible, persons should take Confederate bonds, so as to relieve the government from any pecuniary pressure. You had better not sell your coupons from the bonds, as I understand they are paid in gold, but let the Confederacy keep the gold. Citizens should not receive a cent of gold from the government when it is so scarce. The only objection to parting with your coupons is, that, if they are payable in gold, it will be taking just so much out of the Treasury, when it needs all it has. Give my love and congratulations to William [his brother-in-law, Major W.W. Morrison] upon his promotion. I saw Captain Barringer at Manassas, and his regiment of cavalry presented a fine appearance. I send you a letter announcing that Amy [his faithful old servant] has gone to a better world. The tears came to my eyes more than once while reading it.

NOVEMBER 16, 1861   Don't you tremble when you see that you have to read such a long letter, for I'm going to write it just as full as it can hold. And you wish that I could have my headquarters at Mr. Grigsby's? I tell you this is a much better place for my pet. You can have plenty of society of charming ladies here, and the Rev. Mr. Graham, our Presbyterian minister, lives in the second house from here, his door being only about thirty yards from our gate. This house belongs to Lieutenant Colonel Moore, of the Fourth Virginia Volunteers, and has a large yard around it. The situation is beautiful. The building is of cottage style and contains six rooms. I have two rooms, one above the other. My lower room, or office, has a matting on the floor, a large fine table, six chairs, and a piano. The walls are papered with elegant gilt paper. I don't remember to have ever seen more beautiful papering, and there are five paintings hanging on the walls. If I only had my little woman here, the room would be set off. The upper room is neat, but not a full story, and is, I may say, only remarkable for being heated in a peculiar manner, by a flue from the office below. Through the blessing of our ever-kind Heavenly Father, I am quite comfortable. I have much work to perform, and wouldn't have much time to talk to my darling except at night; but then there is so much pleasant society among the ladies here that you could pass your time very agreeably. I hope to send for you just as soon as I can do so, with the assurance that I am in winter-quarters.

Anna was delighted with the prospect of joining her husband, and she wasted no time leaving for Richmond where she found "an absent-minded old clergyman" to escort her to Winchester. When she alighted from the stagecoach on that cold, dreary day, she could not find the general. She began climbing the long stairway to the hotel. As she reached the platform and looked back, she saw "an officer muffled up in a military overcoat and cap drawn over his eyes following us in rapid pursuit." Suddenly, "a pair of strong arms caught her in the air; the captive's head was thrown back, and she was kissed again & again by her husband." When asked why he didn't step forward at once, he replied that "he wanted to assure himself that it was his own wife, as he didn't want to commit the blunder of kissing anybody else's *esposa*."

Their joyous time together in Winchester was the longest the Jacksons would spend together during the war. Anna spent much time at the Presbyterian manse with the Rev. James Graham's family. General Jackson continued his regular duties as he added new units assigned to his growing army and drilled all of them for the arduous war ahead. To his great delight, the old Stonewall Brigade rejoined their commander.

Chapter Six

DEFENDING HEARTH AND HOME

Much of January 1862 was taken up with a cold and controversial campaign against the Union held towns of Romney and Bath in the mountains, resulting in both victory over his blue clad foes and conflict with subordinate generals. Stonewall Jackson tendered his resignation from the army after several officers disobeyed orders and then appealed to politicians in Richmond behind his back. The resignation was, of course, rejected but had repercussions for the regiments involved.

Anna's stay in Winchester, according to the Reverend Graham "seemed to be the greatest alleviation of Jackson's trials.... His devotion to her was unbounded and he lavished upon her every attention and expression of tenderness."[6] The Jacksons and the Grahams became close friends and confidants and the pastor spent many an evening with the general discussing theology and military affairs. Pastor Graham's reminiscences of the Jackson's winter sojourn in Winchester is a recorded treasure of warm Christian friendship.

General Jackson drilled his men and worked hard with his staff six days a week awaiting spring, anticipating the workings of Providence in renewed conflict. In early March he placed Anna on the road to Richmond and out of the theater of battle. Little did either suspect that their separation would last thirteen months.

A Union army outnumbering Jackson three to one under General Nathaniel Banks began their incremental movements toward Winchester and the little command of Stonewall Jackson. On March 11, the Southern army of about 3,600 men abandoned the city and the Federals moved in. On March 23, Jackson returned and attacked the Union Army at Kernstown, acting on intelligence reports which indicated only one Yankee brigade in the town. The battle, just south of Winchester, began with the hard-hitting verve for which his troops would become universally known. As the day waned, three enemy brigades with more artillery than previously known, struck back, and after suffering heavy casualties, Jackson's force fled the field and retreated up the Shenandoah Valley toward their old camps.

History would show that the fight at Kernstown was a strategic victory for the South since it forced the Federal government to send more troops to the Valley, away from the mighty invasion force under General George B. McClellan that was moving to capture Richmond. Over the next two months, Stonewall Jackson would rewrite the military history books in an audacious and brilliant campaign that is still studied in the military schools of the world.

MARCH 10 1862   My darling, you made a timely retreat from here, for on Friday the Yankees came within five miles of this place. Ashby skirmished for some time with them, and after they fell back he followed them until they halted near Bunker Hill, which is twelve miles from here, where they are at present. The troops are in excellent spirits.... How God does bless us wherever we are! [This was in reference to the kindness he had received in Winchester.] I am very thankful for the measure of health with which He blesses me. I do not remember having been in such good health for years.... My heart is just overflowing with love for my little darling wife.

MARCH 17, 1862, WOODSTOCK   The Federals have possession of Winchester. They advanced upon the town other Friday after you left, but Ashby, aided by a kind Providence, drove them back. I had the other troops under arms, and marched to meet the enemy, but they did not come nearer than about five miles of the town, and fell back to Bunker Hill. On last Tuesday they advanced again, and again our troops were under arms to meet them, but after coming within four miles of the town they halted for the night. I was in hopes that they would advance on me during the evening, as I felt that God would give us the victory; but as they halted for the night, and I knew they could have large reinforcements by morning, I determined to fall back, and sent my troops back the same night to their wagons in rear of Winchester, and the next morning moved still farther to the rear.

MARCH 24, 1862   Yesterday important considerations, in my opinion, rendered it necessary to attack the enemy near Winchester. The action commenced about 3 P.M. and lasted until dark. Our men fought bravely, but the superior numbers of the enemy repulsed me. Many valuable lives were lost. Our God was my shield. His protecting care is an additional cause for gratitude. I lost one piece of artillery and three caissons. The loss of the enemy in killed and wounded was probably superior to ours.

MARCH 28, 1862, MOUNT JACKSON   My little army is in excellent spirits. It feels that it inflicted a severe blow upon the enemy. I stayed in camp last night bivouacking. To-day I am in the house of a Mr. Allen, where I am quite comfortable. This is a beautiful country. The celebrated Meem farm is near here, and is the most magnificent one that I know of anywhere. After God, our God, again blesses us with peace, I hope to visit this country with my darling, and enjoy beauty, and loveliness.

APRIL 7, 1862   My precious pet, your sickness gives me great concern; but so live that it, and all your trials, may be sanctified to you, remembering that "our light afflictions, which are but for a moment, work out for us a far more exceeding and eternal weight of glory," I trust you and all I have in the hands of a kind Providence, knowing that all things work together for the good of His people.

Yesterday was a lovely Sabbath day. Although I had not the privilege of hearing the word of life, yet it felt like a holy Sabbath day, beautiful, serene, and lovely. All it wanted was the church-bell and God's services in the sanctuary to make it complete. . . .

Our gallant little army is increasing in numbers, and my prayer is that it may be an army of the living God as well as of its country.

APRIL 11, 1862   I am very much concerned at having no letter this week, but my trust is in the Almighty. How precious is the consolation flowing from the Christian's assurance that "all things work together for good to them that love God!" . . . God gave us a glorious victory in the Southwest [at Shiloh], but the loss of the great Albert Sidney Johnston is to be mourned. I do not remember having ever felt so sad at the death of a man whom I had never seen. . . . Although I was repulsed in the attempt to recover Winchester, yet the enemy's loss appears to have been three times that of ours. In addition to this, the great object which required me to follow up the enemy, as he fell back from Strasburg, seems to have been accomplished very thoroughly. I am well satisfied with the result. Congress has passed a vote of thanks, and General Johnston has issued a very gratifying order upon the subject, one which will have a fine effect upon my command. The great object to be acquired by the battle demanded time to make known its accomplishments. Time has shown that while the field is in possession of the enemy, the most essential fruits of the battle are ours. For this and all of our Heavenly Father's blessings, I wish I could be ten thousand times more thankful. Should any report be published, my views and object in fighting and its fruits will then become known. You appear much concerned at my attacking *on Sunday*. I was greatly concerned, too; but I felt it my duty to do it, in consideration of the ruinous effects that might result from postponing the battle until the morning. So far as I can see, my course was a wise one; the best that I could do under the circumstances, though very distasteful to my feelings; and I hope and pray to our Heavenly Father that I may never again be circumstanced as on that day. I believed that so far as our troops were concerned, necessity and mercy both called for the battle. I do hope the war will soon be over, and that I shall never again have to take the field. Arms is a profession that, if its principles are adhered to for success, requires an officer to do what he fears may be wrong, and yet, according to military experience, must be done, if success is to be attained. And this fact of its being necessary to success, and being accompanied with success, and that a departure from it is accompanied with disaster, suggests that it must be right. Had I fought the battle on Monday instead of Sunday, I fear our cause would have suffered; whereas, as things turned out, I consider our cause gained much from the engagement.

After the engagement at Kernstown, Jackson reorganized and enlarged his army. Conscription, for which he was vociferously thankful, added new recruits and General Richard S. Ewell's brigades were placed in a strategic position to help him if called upon. General Jackson sacked Richard Garnett, commander of the Stonewall Brigade, a move that many considered tyrannical and unjustified. The Valley commander also added to his staff during March and April: the skillful Keith Boswell and veteran Thomas Williamson as engineers, the tall New Yorker Jedediah Hotchkiss as his official map maker, his youngest staff member Henry Kyd Douglass as aide and assistant adjutant, and finally, his wife's cousin's husband, the estimable Presbyterian theologian Robert Lewis Dabney as adjutant general.

In mid April, the boastful General Nathaniel Banks moved his forces south from Winchester to Harrisonburg. Another Union army marched simultaneously to join him and create a host of around 35,000 men to crush Jackson's potential 16,000. Stonewall concocted a successful plan to trick Banks into thinking the Confederates had left the Valley for Richmond and to turn around and march swiftly against each Federal force and defeat them in detail. He shared the plans of his strategic masterpiece with no one—not his generals, not his staff, not his wife.

APRIL 16, 1862, NEAR NEW MARKET   This morning is warm and spring-like, and this country is one of the most beautiful that I ever beheld. . . . On last Wednesday the enemy advanced on me at one o'clock A.M., and I fell back to this place, where I arrived on Friday. My route was through New Market and Harrisonburg. I am about midway between Harrisonburg and Stannardsville. The enemy did not advance as far as Harrisonburg on the valley turnpike. The advance of the two armies is within a few miles of each other. . . . I do want so much to see my darling, but fear such a privilege will not be enjoyed for some time to come.

APRIL 1862, SWIFT RUN GAP   Dr. Dabney is here, and I am very thankful to God for it. He comes up to my highest expectations as a staff officer.

MAY 5, 1862, STAUNTON   Since I last wrote to my darling I have been very busy. On Wednesday last I left my position near Swift Run Gap, and moved up the south fork of the Shenandoah to Port Republic, which is about three miles from Weyer's Cave. I would like to see the cave, for I remembered that my little pet had been there, and that gave me a deeper interest in the great curiosity. The road up the river was so treacherous that I could only advance about six miles per day, and to leave the road was at the risk of sinking yet deeper in the quicksands, in which that locality abounds. The country is one of the loveliest I have every seen. On Saturday the march was resumed, and we crossed the Blue Ridge at what is known as Brown's Gap, and thus entered into Eastern Virginia. I stopped with a very agreeable family named Pace. Here I expected to pass the Sabbath, but on Sunday morning I received a dispatch stating that part of the enemy's force had arrived within one day's march of Brigadier-General Edward Johnson's camp. Under the circumstances I felt it incumbent upon me to press forward, and I arrived here last evening, where I am stopping at the Virginia House. The troops are still coming in. The corps of cadets of the Virginia Military Institute is here.

The first Union forces to fall victim to Jackson's bold thrust were brigades under the command of Indianian Robert H. Milroy near the village of McDowell on May 8 in Highland Country. The Union soldiers fought bravely, if not skillfully, but at the end of the day, Stonewall Jackson held the field at a cost of twice the casualties of the foe. His report to Richmond was simply "God blessed our arms with victory yesterday."

Having blunted the Union columns marching from the West and intimidated and chased them back into the mountains, Jackson turned his weary troops back toward Staunton in the Valley. Exercizing rigid discipline, the general marched his Confederate troops for five days in the pouring

87

rain, achieving fifteen miles daily. In the near future, the men of Stonewall Jackson's corps would proudly wear the label of "Jackson's foot cavalry."

When Nathaniel Banks divided his army into several separated contingents, Jackson seized the opportunity to surprise the invaders and drive them from the Shenandoah region. On May 23, about a thousand Union soldiers at Front Royal at the northern end of the Luray Valley were the first to find out that Jackson was still in the Valley and were, in fact, swarming down upon them. After a short, sharp fight, the Yankees "ran like sheep," according to one resident of the town. Two days later, the Southern forces caught up to the retreating Banks at Winchester and again drove the Yankees from the field and went whooping after them through the streets of Winchester. A young soldier in the Union army wrote home that "we were two months going down [sic] the Valley after Stonewall Jackson. It was just twenty days getting back with Stonewall after us." With a loss of 400 casualties, Jackson had inflicted about 3,500 casualties on the enemy and captured so many weapons and military stores at Winchester, it took days to count the haul. The medical supplies left behind were greater than those "in the whole Confederacy." Henceforth, the Northern commander was called "Commissary Banks" by the thankful and hungry Confederate soldiers.

Just as in the case of the fight at McDowell, Stonewall Jackson showed up where least expected, struck hard with his exhausted but exultant troops, and did not stop till the enemy was fleeing pell-mell in the opposite direction. The defeat created a panic in the enemy capital, and President Lincoln prevented McDowell's army from reinforcing the invasion force on the Virginia Peninsula, which was inching its way toward Richmond. They were redirected to the Valley to combine with the forces already in the vicinity and destroy Jackson. General Fremont began an eastward march from the mountains around Franklin, Banks reassembled his shaken troops in Harper's Ferry, and General James Shields marched west from Fredericksburg with two divisions. With three armies converging on him, Jackson escaped a potentially disastrous trap set by the enemy and retreated up the Valley. He had been able to get letters off to his wife on May 26 and June 2 but not again until after the final denouncement of the Shenandoah Valley campaign.

MAY 12, 1862, HEADQUARTERS, VALLEY DISTRICT, NEAR FRANKLIN My precious darling, I telegraphed you on the 9th that God had blest us with victory at McDowell. I have followed the enemy to this place, which is about three miles from Franklin. The enemy has been reinforced, and apparently designs making a stand beyond Franklin. I expect to reconnoiter to-day, but do not know as yet whether I will attack him thus reinforced. We have divine service at ten o'clock to-day (Monday) to render thanks to Almighty God for having crowned our arms with success, and to implore His continued favor.

MAY 19, 1862, NEAR HARRISONBURG How I do desire to see our country free and at peace! It appears to me that I would appreciate home more than I have ever done before. Here I am sitting in the open air, writing on my knee for want of a table.... Yesterday Dr. Dabney preached an excellent sermon from the text: "Come unto me, all ye that labor and are heavy laden, and I will give you rest." It is a great privilege to have him with me.

MAY 26, 1862 My precious darling, an ever-kind Providence blest us with success at Front Royal on Friday, between Strasburg and Winchester on Saturday, and here with a successful engagement on yesterday. I do not remember having ever seen such rejoicing as was manifested by the people of Winchester as our army yesterday passed through the town in pursuit of the enemy. The people seemed nearly frantic with joy; indeed, it would be almost impossible to describe their manifestations of rejoicing and gratitude. Our entrance into Winchester was one of the most stirring scenes of my life. The town is much improved in loyalty to our cause. Your friends greatly desired to see you with me. Last night I called to see Mr. and Mrs. Graham, who were very kind.... Time forbids a longer letter, but it does not forbid my loving my esposita.

JUNE 2, 1862 I am again retiring before the enemy. They endeavored to get in my rear by moving on both flanks of my gallant army, but our God has been my guide and saved me from their grasp. You must not expect long letters from me in such busy times as these, but always believe that your husband never forgets his little darling.

A quick glance at a map of the Shenandoah Valley shows the precarious position of Stonewall Jackson's army at the end of May and beginning of June 1862. General Shield's army was slogging its way south through torrential downpours and mud in the Luray Valley between the villages of Luray and Conrad's Store. Freemont's army was in Harrisonburg awaiting a link-up with Shields. Jackson positioned his men at Port Republic, the only place Shields could cross the swollen North River without returning to Luray and Crossing the Massanutten Mountain to New Market and the Valley turnpike.

On Sunday, June 8, Jackson was surprised by a flying column of Union cavalry, who dashed into Port Republic unopposed and came very near capturing the Confederate commander. Major Dabney, who was in bed preparing a sermon, ran outside and began cobbling together any men and artillery he could find to stop the Yankee attack on one of the flanks. The Union attack was successfully repulsed, but it represented only the opening rounds of a continued battle with Shield's infantry the next day. At the same time Confederate General Ewell's division clashed with Freemont's tentative advance several miles away at Cross Keys. The complicated but successful tactical result of fighting both battles and keeping the enemy forces from joining together resulted in a double

Confederate victory. With the retreat of the Union forces, the Valley Campaign of 1862 came to an end.

Although Stonewall Jackson gave the glory to God for all that was accomplished, the newspapers made him a household name across North America. As his wife proudly summarized, "Within forty days he had marched four hundred miles; fought four pitched battles, defeated four separate armies, with numerous combats and skirmishes; sent to the rear three thousand, five hundred prisoners; killed and wounded a still larger number of the enemy, and defeated or neutralized forces three times as numerous as his own upon his proper theatre of war, besides keeping the corps of McDowell inactive at Fredericksburg."

JUNE 10, 1862, NEAR PORT REPUBLIC On Sunday, the 8th, an attack was made upon us by a part of Shields's command about seven o'clock A.M., which a kind Providence enabled us to repulse. During the same morning Fremont attacked us from the opposite side, and after several hours' fight he also was repulsed. Yesterday morning I attacked that part of Shields' force which was near Port Republic, and, after a hotly contested field from near six to ten and a half A.M., completely routed the enemy, who lost eight pieces of artillery during the two days. God has been our shield, and to His name be all the glory. I sent you a telegram yesterday. How I do wish for peace, but only upon the condition of our national independence!

JUNE 14, 1862, NEAR WEYER'S CAVE   When I look at the locality of the cave, I take additional interest in it from the fact that my *esposita* was there once. . . . Our God has again thrown his shield over me in the various apparent dangers to which I have been exposed. This evening we have religious services in the army for the purpose of rendering thanks to the Most High for the victories with which He has crowned our arms, and to offer earnest prayer that He will continue to give us success, until, through His divine blessing, our independence shall be established. Wouldn't you like to get home again?

Chapter Seven

DEFENDING THE CAPITAL

In June of 1862, a Union army under the command of General George B. McClellan, numbering more than 102,000 men, moved into positions across the Virginia countryside a mere nine miles from the Confederate capital. Interposed between the blue host and Richmond stood Robert E. Lee and his army of nearly 72,000. What had begun two months earlier as a meticulous but less than combative march to the front door of the new nation's capital was about to resolve itself in a week of maneuver, attack, and vicious slaughter. General Lee needed Jackson's 18,500 men and he needed them right away.

Jackson secretly marched his men through Rockfish Gap in the Blue Ridge Mountains and bade farewell to the Valley forever. The army of Stonewall Jackson moved into the fields of battle around Richmond. On Monday afternoon, June 23, General Jackson met with Robert E. Lee in their first war council together. The relationship between the two men, that would later include Major General James Longstreet, would develop into a combat team that would drive the enemy from Richmond, take the war into Northern territory, and defeat four Union commanding generals and their armies in succession over the next ten months.

The Seven Days Campaign consisted of a series of pitched battles, which later received the names of Mechanicsville, Gaines's Mill, Savages Station, White Oak Swamp, Frazier's Farm, and Malvern Hill. Stonewall Jackson's performance, like that of many of Lee's subordinates, was characterized by confusion, indecision, and uncoordinated but bloody attacks. Through it all, Jackson suffered from physical exhaustion and fevers that may have clouded his judgment on several occasions.

The positive results of the campaign included capturing huge amounts of supplies and weapons, inflicting thousands of casualties on the enemy, and most importantly, driving the enemy from the gates of Richmond. The cost, however, was hugely expensive in bloodshed and misery. The capital city was transformed into an enormous hospital center.

After the battle, the modest Jackson visited the city and was embarrassed by the acclaim heaped upon him by the people of Richmond and the newspapers. His wife wrote that "he shrank from public notice and applause."

In July, Major Dabney took a leave of absence, which became permanent due to "camp fever." The general confessed to Anna, "It was with tearful eyes that I consented to our separation." Anna's brother, Joseph Morrison, joined Jackson's staff as an aide and would serve him faithfully until his second wound, which cost him his foot.

A new and more arrogant Union general named John Pope took command of a new Union army which had moved to Culpeper, Virginia, just north of the strategically important railhead of Gordonsville. General Lee sent Jackson there in command of 11,000 veteran Confederate troops to keep an eye on the braggart Pope and smite him if opportunity afforded. Anna was alerted to send her letters to Gordonsville "until you hear otherwise."

While at Gordonsville, the general joined the Presbyterian pastor and their household in family worship and when requested, according to Anna, would conduct prayers himself. Pastor Ewing described those services: "There was something very striking in his prayers. He did not pray to men, but to God. His tones were deep, solemn, tremulous. He seemed to realize that he was speaking to Heaven's King. I never heard any one pray who seemed to be pervaded more fully by a spirit of self-abnegation. He seemed to feel more than any man I ever knew the danger of robbing God of the glory due for our success."

JUNE 30, 1862, NEAR WHITE OAK SWAMP BRIDGE An ever-kind Providence has greatly blessed our efforts and given us great reason for thankfulness in having defended Richmond. To-day the enemy is retreating down the Chickahominy towards the James River. Many prisoners are falling into our hands. General D.H. Hill and I are together. I had a wet bed last night, as the rain fell in torrents. I got up about midnight, and haven't seen much rest since. I do trust that our God will soon bless us with an honorable peace, and permit us to be together at home again in the enjoyment of domestic happiness.

You must give fifty dollars for church purposes, and more should you be disposed. Keep an account of the amount, as we must give at least one tenth of our income. I would like very much to see my darling, but hope that God will enable me to remain at the post of duty until, in His own good time, He blesses us with independence. This going home has injured the army immensely.

JULY 8, 1862 When my command arrived at White Oak Swamp bridge we found it broken up by the enemy; but we opened upon the Federal artillery, and succeeded in securing one of their cannons, four caissons, and one battery wagon, in addition to part of a pontoon-bridge train and prisoners. Many prisoners have fallen into our hands, and they really appear gratified at the idea of being taken. I have never seen prisoners so contented.... On Tuesday we had another engagement, in which General D.H. Hill, with his division, accomplished more than any other part of the army. Other troops were sent to support him, but his division may be said to have borne the brunt of the battle, and he was by far the most distinguished officer engaged that day. My position is now about three miles north of James River, and twenty-five miles below Richmond. During the past week I have not been well, have suffered from fever and debility, but through the blessing of an ever-kind Providence I am much better to-day. Last week I received a present of a beautiful summer hat from a lady in Cumberland. Our Heavenly Father gives me friends wherever I go. . . . It would be delightful to see my darling, but we know that all things are ordered for the best.

JULY 1862 If you will vouch for Joseph's [Anna's brother] being an early riser during the remainder of the war, I will give him an aide-ship. I do not want to make an appointment on my staff except of such as are early risers, but if you will vouch for him to rise regularly at dawn, I will offer him the position.

JULY 19, 1862, GORDONSVILLE I have been staying for a few days with Mrs. Barbour, mother-in-law of the Rev. Mr. Ewing, of our church, and have received much kindness from her and her three daughters. My tent opens upon the Blue Ridge in the distance. The wagon-train is moving in front.

JULY 28, 1862, GORDONSVILLE My darling wife, I am just overburdened with work, and I hope you will not think hard at receiving only very short letters from your loving husband. A number of officers are with me, but people keep coming to my tent—though let me say no more. A

Christian should never complain. The apostle Paul said, "I glory in tribulations!" What a bright example for others!

Chapter Eight

GOD IS WITH US

Anna, ever sensitive to her husband's health, wrote Jackson's physician, Dr. Hunter McGuire, the following note: "Sixteen months of uninterrupted mental and physical labor is enough to break down the strongest constitution, but he is so self-sacrificing, and is such a martyr to duty, that if he thinks he cannot be spared from the service, I'm afraid he would sacrifice his life before he would give up. I know he has great confidence in you as a physician, and I appeal to you, Dr., to assist me in persuading him to rest for a short time if indeed you think it necessary."[7] Nothing came of Anna's desire for him to rest a short time.

On August 7, near Cedar Mountain, Jackson sent his command toward Culpeper. They were spoiling for a fight, and the Yankees gave them one "both fierce and stubborn." General Winder, the gallant commander of the Stonewall Brigade, fell mortally wounded, and the Southern troops began to break when a flanking attack struck them. At that crucial moment "the genius of the storm raised his head amidst the tumultuous billows, and in the instant the tide was turned. Jackson appeared in the mid-torrent of the highway, his face flaming with the inspiration of battle: he ordered the batteries . . . to be withdrawn to save them from capture." He then tried to draw his sword, but it stuck. So he lifted it in the air, scabbard and all, "and shouted to the broken troops with a voice higher than the roar of battle: 'Rally, brave men, and press forward! Your general will lead you! Jackson will lead you! Follow me!'" [8]

Jackson designated August 14 as a day of thanksgiving for the victory. Drill was suspended for the day, and the troops were expected to pray and attend services. Ten days later, Lee and Jackson took counsel together and decided to send Jackson on a daring mission deep behind Pope's army to attack the enemy's lifeline, the Orange and Alexandria Railroad near the old Manassas battlefield. If General Pope turned to find Jackson, Lee would fall on him with Longstreet's corps.

And so it happened, Jackson not only interposed himself between Pope and Washington D.C., but he seized and destroyed the main Federal supply depot near Manassas; he then hid nearby while Pope's army hunted for his isolated command. Jackson attacked a Union column along the Warrenton Turnpike near Groveton at 6:30 P.M. on August 29 and thus opened the Second Battle of Manassas. With his 20,000 men identified and pinned to their position, Pope brought his entire army to bear on the Confederates the next day. The most desperate fighting of the war took place in an unfinished railroad bed, and as Jackson's depleted troops ran out of ammunition, they hurled rocks on the Yankee attackers.

It seemed to Jackson's depleted warriors that their last moment had come when Longstreet's corps crushed the Union flank and sent the Federal forces in retreat toward Washington. Again, the cost of the battle was very high, especially for Stonewall Jackson's corps. A number of Christian friends of the Jackson's were killed, including Hugh White, the youngest son of his Lexington pastor.

The pace of the campaign did not slow. The Army of Northern Virginia continued to move north to Frederick, Maryland where General Lee divided his army into several separate commands. Jackson's corps moved to capture Harper's Ferry which was defended by a small Union force.

AUGUST 11, 1862 On last Saturday our God again crowned our arms with victory, about six miles from Culpeper Court-House. I can hardly think of the fall of Brigadier-General C.S. Winder without tearful eyes. Let us all unite more earnestly in imploring God's aid in fighting our battles for us. The thought that there are so many of God's people praying for His blessing upon the army greatly strengthens and encourages me. The Lord has answered their prayers, and my trust is in Him, that He will continue to do so. If God be for us, who can be against us? That He will still be with us and give us victory until our independence shall be established, and that He will make our nation that people whose God is the Lord, is my earnest and oft-repeated prayer. While we attach so much importance to being free from temporal bondage, we must attach far more to being free from the bondage of sin.

AUGUST 25, 1862 The enemy has taken a position, or rather several positions, on the Fauquier side of the Rappahannock. I have only time to tell you how much I love my little pet dove.

SEPTEMBER 1, 1862 We were engaged with the enemy at and near Manassas Junction Tuesday and Wednesday, and again near the battle-field of Manassas on Thursday, Friday, and Saturday; in all of which God gave us the victory. May He ever be with us, and we ever be His devoted people, is my earnest prayer. It greatly encourages me to feel that so many of God's people are praying for that part of our force under my command. The Lord has answered their prayers; He has again placed us across Bull Run; and I pray that He will make our arms entirely successful, and that all the glory will be given to His holy name, and none of it to man. God has blessed and preserved me through His great mercy. On Saturday, Colonel Baylor and Hugh White were both killed, and Willie Preston was mortally wounded.

SEPTEMBER 8, 1862, FREDERICK, MARYLAND Last evening I attended a German Reformed church in Frederick City. I was not quite near enough to hear all the sermon [his modesty had led him to take a back seat], and I regret to say fell asleep; but had I been near enough to hear, would probably not have been so unfortunate. The minister is a gifted one, and the building beautiful. The pews are arranged in a circular form, so that every person faces the pulpit. The town appears to be a charming place, neat and beautiful. The ladies and gentlemen were sitting in front of the doors, and all looked so comfortable, and I may say elegant, according to my ideas, and their enjoyment looked so genuine, that my heart was in sympathy with the surroundings. If such scenes could only surround me in Lexington, how my heart would, under a smiling Providence, rejoice!

SEPTEMBER 15, 1862, HARPER'S FERRY   It is my grateful privilege to write that our God has given us a brilliant victory at Harper's Ferry to-day. Probably nearly eleven thousand prisoners, a great number of small arms, and over sixty pieces of artillery are, through God's blessing, in our possession. The action commenced yesterday, and ended this morning in the capitulation. Our Heavenly Father blesses us exceedingly. I am thankful to say that our loss was small, and Joseph and myself were mercifully protected from harm.

While Jackson rejoiced in the capitulation of Harper's Ferry, the rest of Lee's army was fighting for its life a few miles away at Sharpsburg, Maryland. Jackson joined the commanding general there and directed the Confederate left flank through the bloodiest single day in American history. General McClellan, again in command of the Army of the Potomac, mishandled the opportunity to destroy Lee's army in detail. Both sides suffered more than 10,000 casualties, and the Confederates retreated back to Virginia, thus ending their first invasion of the North. No letters to Anna are known to exist regarding the Battle of Sharpsburg (also known as the Battle of Antietam). Robert Lewis Dabney writes of the general at Sharpsburg, "During this terrible conflict, General Jackson exposed his life with his accustomed imperturbable bravery, and communicating his own indomitable spirit to his men. Yet he said to a Christian comrade that on no day of battle had he ever felt so calm an assurance that he should be preserved from all personal harm through the protection of his Heavenly Father." [9]

Chapter Nine

REJOICING IN PROVIDENCE

The Confederate army returned to camps near Winchester for the next couple months before taking positions around Fredericksburg in late November. General Jackson's letters of that period reflect his continuing love for God and for his wife, and new daughter, Julia, who was born in November in North Carolina. His values and priorities had not changed one iota since he left home for the war.

During the next period of recovery and refitting the army, General Lee recommended Stonewall Jackson for promotion to lieutenant general and corps command, both of which were granted, and thus he assumed charge over half of the Army of Northern Virginia. Although he was involved in a number of controversies with other officers and was held in contempt by some of them, his popularity with the soldiers reached an all-time high. "A Georgia sergeant in one of Longstreet's regiments noted of the post-Antietam period: 'One day ... I heard cheering down the road in our front. Some of the boys thought it was Stonewall Jackson or a rabbit. . . . Everyone made for the road and sure enough, it was Gen. Jackson galloping along the road with his escort. He passed us with his cap off and the cheering continued down the line as far as we could hear. . . . He certainly creates more excitement than all of the rest of the officers put together.'" [10]

OCTOBER 6, 1862, BUNKER HILL   I am glad that you were privileged to keep Thanksgiving Day. We did not enjoy that blessing, I regret to say. I trust it was generally observed, and that rich blessings may flow from it through our ever-kind Heavenly Father. I also hope that on that day large contributions were made to our Bible Society. You and I have, as you say, special reason for gratitude to God for His goodness and mercy to us. . . . The citizens of Frederick did not present me the horse, as was published, though a Marylander gave me a fine-looking animal, possessed of great muscle and fine powers of endurance; but he was not gentle, and of this the donor notified me. Notwithstanding the notice, I mounted and rode him that evening, and he did well. The next morning, however, when I attempted again to ride him, he reared up and fell back with me, hurting me considerably. Miss Osbourn, of Jefferson, sent me some excellent socks, and a beautiful scarf which I wish my darling had. Our friend, Mrs. Graham, of Winchester, sent me two nice sponge-cakes last week, and a Mr.

Vilwig, of the same place, sent me an excellent arm-chair for camp use. I wish I could keep it until the close of the war, as I think my *esposa* would enjoy it. You are earnestly remembered in my prayers.

OCTOBER 13, 1862, NEAR WINCHESTER   I am sitting in my tent, about twelve miles from our "war-home," where you and I spent such a happy winter. The weather is damp, and for the past two days has been rainy and chilly. Yesterday was communion at Mr. Graham's church, and he invited me to be present, but I was prevented from enjoying that privilege. However, I heard an excellent sermon from the Rev. Dr. Stiles. His text was 1st Timothy, chap. ii. 5th and 6th verses. It was a powerful exposition of the Word of God; and when he came to the word "himself" he placed an emphasis upon it, and gave it a force which I had never felt before, and I realized that, truly, the sinner who does not, under Gospel privileges, turn to God deserves the agonies of perdition. The doctor several times, in appealing to the sinner, repeated the verse—"Who gave himself a ransom for all, to be testified in due time." What more could God do than to give himself a ransom? Dr. Stiles is a great revivalist, and is laboring in a work of grace in General Ewell's division. It is a glorious thing to be a minister of the Gospel of the Prince of Peace. There is no equal position in this world.

Colonel Blanton Duncan, of Kentucky, has presented me with two fine field or marine glasses. He has apparently taken a special interest in me.

OCTOBER 20, 1862, NEAR WINCHESTER Although I greatly desire to see our much-prized Winchester friends, it has not been my privilege to visit the town since last May.... Last night was very cold, but my good friend Dr. Hunter McGuire secured a camp-stove for me, and in consequence, to-day, I am comparatively quite comfortable. Don't send me any more socks, as the kind ladies have given me more than I could probably wear out in two years. God, through kind friends, is showering blessings upon me.... Let the soldiers have all your blankets. [This order was fulfilled, and finally all Stonewall's carpets were sent to the army as covering for the suffering soldiers.]

Don't trouble yourself about representations that are made of your husband. These things are earthly and transitory. There are real and glorious blessings, I trust, in reserve for us beyond this life. It is best for us to keep our eyes fixed upon the throne of God and the realities of a more glorious existence beyond the verge of time. It is gratifying to be beloved and to have our conduct approved by our fellow-men, but this is not worthy to be compared with the glory that is in reservation for us in the presence of our glorified Redeemer. Let us endeavor to adorn the doctrine of Christ our Saviour in all things, knowing that there awaits us a far more exceeding and eternal weight of glory. I would not relinquish the slightest diminution of that glory for this world can give. My prayer is that such may ever be the feeling of my heart. It appears to me that it would be better for you not to have anything written about me. Let us follow the teaching of inspiration—"Let another man praise thee, and not thine own mouth: a stranger, and not thine own lips." I appreciate the loving interest that prompted such a desire in my precious darling.... You have not forgotten my little intimation that we might meet before the end of the year, but I am afraid now that your *esposo* will not be able to leave his command. However, all this is in the hands of the Most High, and my prayer is that He will direct all for His own glory. Should I be prevented from going to see my precious little wife, and mother should grow worse, I wish you to remain with her. In addition to the comfort it would give her, it would also gratify me to know that she was comforted by your being with her. She has my prayers that it may please our Heavenly Father to restore her again to perfect health. Do not send me any more handkerchiefs, socks, or gloves, as I trust I have enough to last until peace. You think you can remember the names of all the ladies who make presents to me, but you haven't heard near all of them. An old lady in Tennessee, of about eighty years, sent me a pair of socks. A few days since a friend in Winchester presented me with a beautiful bridle and martingale for a general officer, according to the Army Regulations. Mr. Porter, of Jefferson, sent me a toll of gray cloth for a suit of clothes, and friends are continually sending things to contribute to my comfort. I mention all this merely to show you how much kindness has been shown me, and to give you renewed cause for gratitude. If I only had you with me in my evenings, it would be such a comfort! I hope it may be my privilege to be in Winchester this winter. The people are so kind, and take a great interest in my *esposita*, and that gratifies me. . . . I am in a Sibley tent, which is of a beautiful conical shape, and I am sure you would enjoy being in it for a while.

NOVEMBER 10, 1862 Colonel A.R. Boteler telegraphs me from Richmond that arrangements are made for supplying my command with blankets. Yesterday about seventeen hundred and fifty were distributed in Winchester. There has been much suffering in my command for want of blankets and shoes, especially the latter.

NOVEMBER 11, 1862 Tell Colonel E—— that I am glad to see he has so pleasant a post as Charlotte, and that *I* would rather be stationed there than anywhere else in the Confederacy. Colonel Boteler deserves the lasting gratitude of the country for having done so much towards clothing our men.

NOVEMBER 17, 1862 I am more concerned again about clothing, especially shoes and blankets, than I expected to be, from what I heard. Colonel Boteler is doing much, and has been the means of greatly contributing to the comfort of our men.... Our gracious Heavenly Father strikingly manifests his kindness to me by disposing people to bestow presents upon me.

NOVEMBER 20, 1862 Don't you wish you were here in Winchester? Our headquarters are about one hundred yards from Mr. Graham's, in a large white house back of his, and in full view of our last winter's quarters, where my *esposa* used to come up and talk with me. Wouldn't it be nice for you to be here again? But I don't know how long you could remain.... I hope to have the privilege of joining in prayer for peace at the time you name, and trust that all our Christian people will; but peace should not be the chief object of prayer in our country. It should aim more especially to implore God's forgiveness of our sins, and make our people a holy people. If we are but His, all things shall work together for the good of our country, and no good thing will He withhold from it.

Chapter Ten

ANSWERS TO PRAYER

God blessed the Jackson's with a healthy baby girl on November 23. The general did not want the announcement made by telegram, so the first he heard of the birth came from a letter from his little daughter, compliments of her aunt. Mother and baby had been the objects of his fervent prayer for many months and with great joy he gave thanks to God.

NOVEMBER 1862   If you had been in Winchester when I commenced this letter, you would not be there now, for your husband is no longer there, but his heart is with his little darling. Write to me at Gordonsville, as I hope to be there by Thursday.

My own dear Father, as my mother's letter has been cut short by my arrival, I think it but justice that I should continue it. I know that you are rejoiced to hear of my coming, and I hope that God has sent me to radiate your pathway through life. I am a very tiny little thing. I weigh only eight and a half pounds, and Aunt Harriet says I am the express image of my darling papa, and so does our kind friend, Mrs. Osborne, and this greatly delights my mother. My aunts both say that I am a little beauty. My hair is dark and long, my eyes are blue, my nose straight just like papa's, and my complexion not all red like most young ladies of my age, but a beautiful blending of the lily and the rose. Now, all this would sound very vain if I were older, but I assure you I have not a particle of feminine vanity, my only desire in life being to nestle in close to my mamma, to feel her soft caressing touch, and to drink in the pearly stream provided by a kind Providence for my support. My mother is very comfortable this morning. She is anxious to have my name decided upon, and hopes you will write and give me a name, with your blessing. We look for my grandmother to-morrow, and expect before long a visit from my little cousin, Mary Graham Avery, who is one month my senior. I was born on Sunday, just after the morning services at church, but I believe my aunt wrote you all about the first day of my life, and this being only the second, my history may be comprised in a little space. But my friends, who are about me like guardian angels, hope for me a long life of happiness and holiness and a futurity of endless bliss.

"Your dear little wee Daughter."

DECEMBER 4, 1862   O! How thankful I am to our kind Heavenly Father for having spared my precious wife and given us a little daughter! I cannot tell you how gratified I am, nor how much I wish I could be with you and see my two darlings. But while this pleasure is denied me, I am thankful it is accorded to you to have the little pet, and I hope it may be a great deal of company and comfort to its mother. Now don't exert yourself to write me, for to know that you were taxing yourself to write would give me more pain than the letter would pleasure, so you must not do it. But you must love your *esposo* in the meantime. . . . I suppose you are just made up now with that baby. Don't you wish your husband wouldn't claim any part of it, but let you have the sole ownership? Don't you regard it as the most precious little creature in the world? Do not spoil it, and don't let anybody tease it. Don't permit it to have a bad temper. How I would love to see the darling little thing? Give her many kisses for her father.

At present I am about fifty miles from Richmond, and one mile from Guiney's Station, on the railroad from Richmond to Fredericksburg. Should I remain here, I do hope you and baby can come to see me before spring, as you can come on the railroad. Wherever I go, God gives me kind friends. The people here show me great kindness. I receive invitation after invitation to dine out, and spend the night, and a great many provisions are sent me, including nice cakes, tea, loaf-sugar, etc., and the socks and gloves and handkerchiefs still come!

I am so thankful to our ever-kind Heavenly Father for having so improved my eyes as to enable me to write at night. He continually showers blessings upon me; and that you should have been spared, and our darling little daughter given us, fills my heart with overflowing gratitude. If I know my unworthy self, my desire is to live entirely and unreservedly to God's glory. Pray, my darling, that I may so live."

Thank sister H—— very kindly, and give the baby-daughter a shower of kisses from her father, and tell her that he loves her better than all the baby-boys in the world, and more than all the other babies in the world.

DECEMBER 10, 1862 This morning I received a charming letter from my darling little daughter, Julia. Do not set your affections upon her, except as a gift from God. If she absorbs too much of our hearts, God may remove her from us.

Chapter Eleven

CHRIST IN THE CAMPS

A braham Lincoln gave command of the Army of the Potomac to Ambrose Burnside after General McClellan failed to pursue and destroy the invading Confederate Army after the Battle of Sharpsburg. Admitting his own inability to handle such an enormous task, Burnside nonetheless acceded to the President's wishes and brought the renewed Federal Army to the environs of Fredericksburg. On the morning of December 11, one hundred and fifty Union artillery pieces opened fire on the town and the hills above it from across the Rappahannock River. As the fog lifted on the morning of December 16, part of the huge Federal army was filing into position below Jackson's position on the right of the Confederate line. Except for briefly piercing Jackson's line, the brave Union soldiers were mowed down in waves in uncoordinated attacks against a well-fortified Confederate line. The retreat of the Yankee army back across the river signaled the end of campaigning until the spring of 1863.

True to form, President Lincoln promoted another general to command the army, Fighting Joe Hooker, who had proved himself aggressive and competent in previous battles.

During the winter of 1862-63, thousands of soldiers in the Confederate camps around Fredericksburg attended worship services held throughout the regiments and brigades of Lee's army. Many hundreds of men professed faith in Christ and many hundreds more were renewed in their Christian faith. The great revival was confined to no one sect, for chaplains and evangelists of every Protestant denomination preached the Gospel for all to hear. Christian officers encouraged the army pastors with prayer, testimony, and attendance at meetings. It is no surprise that Stonewall Jackson was in the forefront of support in the propagation of the Gospel. He told his pastor of the need for more chaplains and allowed his views disseminated in the denominational press. He requested more tracts and Bibles for distribution by colporters. He prayed with the chaplains for the Holy Spirit to bring salvation to the troops, and he attended many meetings, sitting among the men of his command. The revival was powerful, broad, and deep; and Jackson rejoiced in the Lord's work being accomplished among thousands of gray clad soldiers, many of whom would die in the coming year.

DECEMBER 16, 1862   Yesterday, I regret to say, I did not send you a letter. I was on the front from before dawn until after sunset. The enemy, through God's blessing, was repulsed at all points on Saturday, and I trust that our

Heavenly Father will continue to bless us. We have renewed reason for gratitude to Him for my preservation during the last engagement. We have to mourn the deaths of Generals Maxey Gregg and Thomas R.R. Cobb. The enemy has recrossed to the north side of the Rappahannock. . . . I was made very happy at hearing through my baby daughter's last letter that she had entirely recovered, and that she "no longer saw the doctor's gray whiskers." I was much gratified to learn that she was beginning to notice and smile when caressed. I tell you, I would love to caress her and see her smile. Kiss the little darling for her father and give my grateful love to sister H——.

DECEMBER 18, 1862 Our headquarters are now about twelve miles below Fredericksburg, near the house of Mr. Richard Corbin, which is one of the most beautiful buildings I have seen in this country. It is said to have cost sixty thousand dollars. Night before last I was about to spend the night in the woods, but sent to ask if we could procure our supper at the house. Mr. Corbin was absent, serving as a private in the Virginia cavalry, but Mrs. Corbin bountifully supplied us, and requested me to spend the night at her house, which invitation was thankfully accepted, and I had a delightful night's rest. The next morning she urged me to remain, and offered me a neat building in the yard for my office, but I declined, and am now about five hundred yards from the house, encamped in the woods. She told me that if at any time I needed house room, she could let me have it. [He afterwards moved into the office in the yard, and spent most of the time he was in winter-quarters there.]

Baby's letters are read with great interest, and it does her father's heart great good to read them.... I have much work before me, and to-day I expect to commence in earnest. The reports of the battles of McDowell, Winchester, Port Republic, Richmond, Manassas, the Maryland Campaign, Harper's Ferry, and Fredericksburg have all yet to be written. But something has been done towards several of them by my staff.

CHRISTMAS 1862 Yesterday I received the baby's letter with its beautiful lock of hair. How I do want to see that precious baby! And I do earnestly pray for peace. Oh that our country was such a Christian, God-fearing people as it should be! Then might we very speedily look for peace. Last evening I received a letter from Dr. Dabney, saying: "One of the highest gratifications both Mrs. Dabney and I could enjoy would be another visit from Mrs. Jackson when her health is re-established," and he invites me to meet you there. He and Mrs. Dabney are very kind, but it appears to me that it is better for me to remain with my command so long as the war continues, if our gracious Heavenly Father permits. The army suffers immensely by absentees. If all our troops, officers and men, were at their posts, we might, through God's blessing, expect a more speedy termination of the war. The temporal affairs of some are so deranged as to make a strong plea for their returning home for a short time; but our God has greatly blessed me and mine during my absence; and whilst it would be a great comfort to see you and our darling little daughter, and others in whom I take special interest, yet duty appears to require me to remain with my command. It is important that those at headquarters set an example by remaining at the post of duty.

Dr. Dabney writes: "Our little prayer-meeting is still meeting daily to pray for our army and leaders." This prayer-meeting may be the means of accomplishing more than an army. I wish that such existed everywhere. How it does cheer my heart to hear of God's people praying for our cause and for me! I greatly prize the prayers of the pious.

DECEMBER 29, 1862 Yesterday I had the privilege of attending divine service in a church near General Hill's headquarters, and enjoyed the services very much. Dr. White says in a recent letter that our pew at home has been constantly occupied by Wheeling refugees. I am gratified to hear it. He also adds, "How we would rejoice to see you and our dear friend, Mrs. Jackson, again in that pew, and in the lecture-room at prayer-meetings! We still meet every Wednesday afternoon to pray for our army, and especially for our general." May every needful blessing rest upon you and our darling child is the earnest prayer of your devoted husband.

Chapter Twelve

STONEWALL THE FATHER

General Jackson was known for his great fondness for children, and in the first months of 1863, he spent many hours at the Corbin home and played games with little Janie Corbin. Her death was a grief to him. He wrote several tender letters to his wife and baby, longing to be with them again. He sent home child-rearing advice, loving but firm, and always trusting in the Providence of God to accomplish his will in their lives.

JANUARY OR FEBRUARY 1863 I never wrote you about the bereavement of my kind friend Mrs. Corbin. She had an only daughter, probably about five or six years old, and one of the most attractive, if not the most so, that I ever saw at that age. A short time before I left there, the little girl was taken sick with scarlet fever, but appeared to be doing well. I called to see Mrs. Corbin the evening before leaving, and talked to her of her little daughter, whom I supposed to be out of danger, and she too appeared to think so; but the next morning she was taken very ill, and in a few hours died of malignant scarlet fever. There were two other little children, cousins of little Janie, who were staying at the same house, and both of them died of the same disease in a few days. . . . [Anna's sister, Mrs. Avery lost her first-born child as well.] We can sympathize with her, and I wish I could comfort her, but no human comfort can fully meet her case; only the Redeemer can, and I trust that she finds Jesus precious, most precious, in this her sad hour of trial. Give my tenderest love and sympathy to her.

JANUARY 5, 1863 How much I do want to see you and our darling baby! But I don't know when I shall have this happiness, as I am afraid, since hearing so much about the little one's health, that it would be imprudent to bring it upon a journey, so I must just content myself. Mrs. General Longstreet, Mrs. General A.P. Hill, and Mrs. General Rodes have all been to see their husbands. Yesterday I saw Mrs. Rodes at church, and she looked so happy that it made me wish I had Mrs. Jackson here too; but whilst I cannot see my wife and baby, it is a great comfort to know that you have a darling little pet to keep you company in my absence. . . . I heard a good sermon at Grace Church (where General Hill has his headquarters) by an Episcopal minister, Mr. Friend.

Colonel Faulkner is with us again, and I expect him to take the position of my senior adjutant-general.

JANUARY 6, 1863 I am very thankful to our kind Heavenly Father for good tidings from you and baby— specially that she is restored again to health, and I trust that we all three may so live as most to glorify His holy name. . . . I have a visor, but I hope I shall not have to sleep in a tent any more this winter. My ears are still troubling me, but I am very thankful that my hearing is as good as usual, and from my appearance one would suppose that I was perfectly well. Indeed, my health is essentially good, but I do not think I shall be able further to stand what I have already stood, although, with the exception of the increased sensitiveness of my ears, my health has improved. I am sorry to hear that dear mother's health does not improve. . . . We have several cases of smallpox at Guiney's, and I expect you will have to give up all idea of coming to see me until spring, as I fear it would be too much of a risk for you and baby to travel up here.

The other day I received from the citizens of Augusta County a magnificent horse, with an excellent saddle and bridle. It is the most complete riding equipment that I have seen. My kind friends went so far as to get patent stirrups, constructed so as to open and throw the foot from the stirrup in the event of the rider being thrown and the foot hung in the stirrups. How kind is God to us! Oh that I were more grateful!

JANUARY 17, 1863 Yesterday I had the pleasure of receiving a letter from my *esposita* four days after it was written. Doesn't it look as if Confederate mails are better than United States mails? Don't you remember how long it took for letters to come from Charlotte to Lexington under the old *regime*? I derived an additional pleasure in reading a letter from the conviction that it has not traveled on the Sabbath. How delightful will be our heavenly home, where everything is sanctified! . . . I am gratified at hearing that you have commenced disciplining the baby. Now be careful, and don't let her conquer *you.* She must not be permitted to have that will of her own, of which you speak. How I would love to see the little darling, whom I love so tenderly, though I have never seen her; and if the war were only over, I tell you, I would hurry down to North Carolina to see my wife and baby. I have much work to do. Lieutenant Colonel Faulkner is of great service to me in making out my reports. Since he is my senior adjutant-general, Pendleton is promoted to a majority, and is the junior adjutant-general. Major Bier, my chief of ordnance, has been ordered to Charleston, and Captain William Allan, of Winchester, is his successor. Colonel Smeade is my inspector-general, so you must not complain of my not writing to you about my staff. I regret to see our Winchester friends again in the hands of the enemy. I trust that, in answer to prayer, our country will soon be blessed with peace. If we were only that obedient people that we should be, I would, with increased confidence, look for a speedy termination of hostilities. Let us pray more and live more to the glory of God. . . . I am still thinking and thinking about that baby, and do want to see her. Can't you send her to me by express? There is an express line all the way to Guiney's. I am glad to hear that she sleeps well at night, and doesn't disturb her mother. But it would be better not to call her a cherub; no earthly being is such. I am also gratified that Hetty is doing well. Remember me to her, and tell her that, as I didn't give her a present last Christmas, I intend giving her two next. . . . Don't you accuse my baby of not being *brave*. I do hope she will get over her fear of strangers. If, before strangers take her, you would give them something to please her, and thus make her have pleasant associations with them, and seeing them frequently, I trust she would lose her timidity. It is gratifying that she is growing so well, and I am thankful she is so bright and knowing. I do wish I could see her funny little ways, and hear her "squeal out with delight" at seeing the little chickens. I am sometimes afraid that you will make such an idol of that baby that God will take her from us. Are *you* not afraid of it? Kiss her for her father.

I have this morning received two presents—a pair of gauntlets from near the Potomac, and another beautiful pair from Mrs. Preston Trotter, of Brownsburg. A kind gentleman, Mr. Stephens, of Nelson County, sent me a barrel of select pippins.

JANUARY 31, 1863   Captain Bushby, of the British Army, called to see me to-day, and presented me with a water-proof oil-cloth case in which to sleep on a wet night in summer campaigning. I can encase myself in it, keep dry, and get a good night's sleep.

Chapter Thirteen

VICISSITUDES OF LIFE

S tonewall Jackson was probably the best known soldier on
the planet in 1863, and many people sent him gifts. His
popularity did not distract him from his duties though, and
as the campaign season approached, he continued sharpening
the skills of his soldiers and attending to the minutia of
military life. He continued to delight in his daughter though
separated by many miles. He also rejoiced that the Sabbath
days could now be kept regularly and deeply appreciated the
preaching and prayer meetings of the army.

FEBRUARY 3, 1863   In answer to the prayers of God's
people, I trust He will soon give us peace. I haven't seen
my wife for nearly a year—my home in nearly two years,
and have never seen our darling little daughter; but it is
important that I, and those at headquarters, should set an
example of remaining at the post of duty. Joseph would like
very much to go home, but unless mother gets worse, he

had better not. . . . My old Stonewall Brigade has built a log church. As yet I have not been in it. I am much interested in reading Hunter's *Life of Moses*. It is a delightful book, and I feel more improved in reading it than by an ordinary sermon. I am thankful to say that my Sabbaths are passed more in meditation than formerly. Time thus spent is genuine enjoyment.

FEBRUARY 7, 1863 This has been a beautiful spring day. I have been thinking lately about gardening. If I were at home, it would be time for me to begin to prepare the hot-bed. Don't you remember what interest we used to take in our hot-bed? If we should be privileged to return to our old home, I expect we would find many changes. An ever-kind Providence is showering blessings down upon me. Yesterday Colonel M.G. Harman and Mr. William J. Bell, jun., of Staunton, presented me with an excellent horse. As yet I have not mounted him, but I saw another person ride him, and I hope soon to have that pleasure myself. . . . Just to think our baby is nearly three months old. Does she notice and laugh much? You have never told me how much she looks like her mother. I tell you, I want to know how she looks. If you could hear me talking to my *esposa* in the mornings and evenings, it would make you laugh, I'm sure. It is funny the way I talk to her when she is hundreds of miles away. . . . Jim has returned from Lexington, and brought a letter from "Cy" [a Negro servant], asking permission to take unto himself a wife, to which I intend to give my consent, provided you or his mother do not object. . . . I am so much concerned about mother's health as to induce me to recommend a leave of absence for Joseph. I send this note by him, and also send the baby a silk handkerchief. I have thought that as it is brightly colored, it might attract her attention. Remember, it is her first present from her father, and let me know if she notices it.

FEBRUARY 14, 1863 Your delightful letter of six pages received a welcome reception this evening. I am thankful to see that our kind Heavenly Father is again restoring mother to health. I felt uneasy about her, and thought that Joseph had better make a visit home. I have made the restoration of mother's health a subject of prayer; but then we know that our dear ones are mortal, and that God does not always answer prayer according to our erring feelings. I think that if, when we see ourselves in a glass, we should consider that all of us that is visible must turn to corruption and dust, we would learn more justly to appreciate the relative importance of the body that perishes and the soul that is immortal. . . . Your accounts of baby are very gratifying, and intensify my desire to see her. If peace is not concluded before next winter, I do hope you can bring her and spend the winter with me. This would be very delightful. If we are spared, I trust an ever-kind Providence will enable us to be together all winter. I am glad little Julia was pleased with her present, and wish I could have seen her laugh. . . . I do serve the 27th of next month as a day of humiliation, prayer, and fasting, as our President has designated in his proclamation. To-morrow is the Sabbath. My Sabbaths are looked forward to with pleasure. I don't know that I ever enjoyed Sabbaths as I do this winter. . . . I don't think I have written you about recent presents. About a week since, I received from Mr. W.F. De la Rue, of London, a superb English saddle, bridle, holsters, saddle-cover, blankets, whip, spurs, etc.—the most complete riding equipage that I have seen for many a day. Its completeness is remarkable. This evening I received from Mr. John Johnson, of London, a box containing two flannel shirts, two pairs of long woolen stockings extending above the knees, a buckskin shirt, a pair of boots, a pair of leather leggings extending about eight inches above the knees, two pairs of excellent fitting leather gloves, and a very superior variegated colored blanket. Our ever-kind Heavenly Father gives me friends among strangers. He is the source of every blessing, and I desire to be more grateful to Him.

MARCH 7, 1863   I have just finished my report of the battle of McDowell. . . . There is a good deal of religious interest in the army. Rev. Mr. Lacy is with me now, and I expect will continue with the army during the war. Rev. William J. Hoge is chaplain of the Second Regiment of Virginia Volunteers. If you were here you would find a number of friends.

Chapter Fourteen

THE FINAL DAYS

As the spring campaign season approached, General Jackson longed more and more to see his family. In the Providence of God, he was introduced to his little daughter when Anna and Julia were able to visit him for nine days. They spent many glorious hours together at their comfortable accommodations at the Yerby home.

MARCH 14, 1863 The time has about come for campaigning, and I hope early next week to leave my room, and go into a tent near Hamilton's Crossing, which is on the railroad, about five miles from Fredericksburg. It is rather a relief to get where there will be less comfort than in a room, as I hope thereby persons will be prevented from encroaching so much upon my time. I am greatly behind in my reports, and am very desirous to get through with them before another campaign commences. Do you remember when my little wife used to come up to my headquarters in Winchester and talk with her *esposo?* I would love to see her sunny face peering into my room again.... On next Monday there is to be a meeting of the chaplains of my corps, and I pray that good may result.... I am now in camp, but I do not know of any house near by where you could be accommodated, should you come; and, moreover, I might not be here when you would arrive, as the season for campaigning has come. Before this time last year, the campaign had begun, and so far as we can see, it may begin again at any time. The movements of the enemy must influence ours, and we can't say where we shall be a week hence.

APRIL 10, 1863   I trust that God is going to bless us with great success, and in such a manner as to show that it is all His gift; and I trust and pray that it will lead our country to acknowledge Him, and to live in accordance with His will as revealed in the Bible. There appears to be an increased religious interest among our troops here. Our chaplains have weekly meetings on Tuesdays; and the one of this week was more charming than the preceding one.

APRIL 18, 1863   I am beginning to look for my darling and my baby. I shouldn't be surprised to hear at any time that they were coming, and I tell you there would be one delighted man. Last night I dreamed that my little wife and I were on opposite sides of a room, in the center of which was a table. And the little baby started from her mother, making her way along under the table, and finally reached her father. And what do you think she did when she arrived at her destination? She just climbed up on her father and kissed him! And don't you think he was a happy man? But when he awoke he found it all a delusion. I am glad to hear that she enjoys out-doors, and grows, and coos, and laughs. How I would love to see her sweet ways! That her little chubby hands have lost their resemblance to mine is not regretted by me. . . . Should I write to you to have any more pantaloons made for me, please do not have much gold braid about them. I became so ashamed of the broad gilt band that was on the cap you sent as to induce me to take it off. I like simplicity.

April 20, 1863 Yesterday I received you letter, but you did not say a word about coming to see your *esposo.* I do hope that ere this you have received mine, saying you could come, and that you at once got an escort and started. There is no time for hesitation if you have not started. There is increasing probability that I may be elsewhere as the season advances. But don't come unless you get a good escort. I am not certain that I can get accommodations for you; but I don't think there will be any difficulty about it, as I hope some kind neighbor would try to make us comfortable for the short time that you remain. I think that we might get in at Mr. Yerby's, which is less than a mile from my headquarters.

That was the last letter Stonewall Jackson sent to his beloved wife Anna, for she indeed came to him at last, arriving on Monday, April 20. Years later she told of their arrival and visit:

Little Julia was nearly five months old now, and was plump, rosy, and good, and with her nurse, Hetty, we set out upon this visit, so full of interest and anticipated joys. . . . Hetty and I were all anxious to have our baby present her best appearance for her father's first sight of her, and she could not have better realized our wishes. She awoke from a long, refreshing sleep just before the train stopped, and never looked more bright and charming. When he entered the coach to receive us, his rubber overcoat was dripping from the rain which was falling, but his face was all sunshine and gladness; and, after greeting his wife, it was a picture, indeed, to see his look of perfect delight and admiration as his eyes fell upon that baby! She was at the lovely, smiling age; and catching his eager look of supreme interest in her, she beamed her brightest and sweetest smiles upon him in return, so it seemed to be a mutual fascination. He was afraid to take her in his arms, with his wet overcoat; but as we drove in a carriage to Mr. Yerby's, his face reflected all the happiness and delight that were in his heart, and he expressed much surprise and gratification at her size and beauty. Upon our arrival at the house he speedily divested himself of his overcoat, and, taking his baby in his arms, he caressed her with the tenderest affection, and held her long and lovingly. During the whole of this short visit, when he was with us, he rarely had her out of his arms, walking her, and amusing her in every way that he could think of—sometimes holding her up before a mirror and saying, admiringly, "Now, Miss Jackson, look at yourself!" Then he would turn to an old lady of the family and say: "Isn't she a *little gem*?" He was frequently told that she resembled him, but he would say: "No, she is too pretty to look like me." When she slept in the day, he would often kneel over her cradle, and gaze upon her little face with the most rapt admiration, and he said he felt almost as if she were an angel, in her innocence and purity. I have often wished that the picture which was presented to me of that father kneeling over the cradle of that lovely infant could have been put upon canvas. And yet with all his fondness and devotion to the little lady, he had no idea of spoiling her, as will be seen by his undertaking to teach her a lesson in self-control before she was five months old! One day she began to cry to be taken from the bed on which she was lying, and as soon as her wish was gratified, she ceased to cry. He laid her back upon the bed, and the crying was renewed with increased violence. Of course, the mother-heart wished to stop this by taking her up again, but her exclaimed: "This will never do!" and commanded "all hands off" until that little will of her own should be conquered. So there she lay, kicking and screaming, while he stood over her with as much coolness and determination as if he were directing a battle; and he was true to the name of Stonewall, even in disciplining a baby! When she stopped crying he would take her up, and if she began to cry again he would lay her down again, and this he kept up until finally she was completely conquered, and became perfectly quiet in his hands. . . .

The next Sabbath [April 30] was a most memorable one to me, being the last upon which I was privileged to attend divine service with my husband on earth, and to worship in camp with such a company of soldiers as I had never seen together in a religious congregation. My husband took me in an ambulance to his headquarters, where the services were held, and on the way were seen streams of officers and soldiers, some riding, some walking, all wending their way to the place of worship. Arrived there, we found Mr. Lacy in a tent, in which we were seated, together with General Lee and other distinguished officers. I remember how reverent and impressive was General Lee's bearing, and how handsome he looked, with his splendid figure and faultless military attire. In front of the tent, under the canopy of heaven, were spread out in dense masses the soldiers, sitting upon benches or standing. The preaching was earnest and edifying, the singing one grand volume of song, and the attention and good behavior of the assembly remarkable. That Sabbath afternoon my husband spent entirely with me, and his conversation was more spiritual than I had ever observed before. He seemed to be giving utterance to those religious meditations in which he so much delighted. He never appeared to be in better health than at this time, and I never saw him look so handsome and noble.

On the morning of April 29, a courier came to the Yerby farm with the news that the Union army was crossing the river, a signal that Hooker intended to turn the Confederate Army out of their positions in Fredericksburg. As the artillery thundered in the distance, General Jackson told Anna to prepare to leave on the next train to Richmond. A few hours later, he sent a note to Anna "explaining why he could not leave his post and invoking God's care and blessing upon us in our sudden departure, and especially was he tender and loving in his mention of the baby."

General Lee and his army were in a very precarious position. Longstreet's corps was still near Suffolk, Virginia, far from the Fredericksburg area. Joseph Hooker had not been idle over the winter months; the Union army of 134,000 was fit and ready, morale was high, and his plan seemed to contain no weaknesses. He boasted to President Lincoln that "my plans are perfect, and when I seek to carry them out, may God have mercy on General Lee, for I will have none." He then marched his army into the most tangled and inaccessible woods in central Virginia. Visibility was near zero in many places, and the narrow paths and small clearings contributed little to maneuverability especially for cavalry which were necessary for scouting and intelligence. And he was facing two generals, Lee and Jackson, who were unafraid to leave him begging for mercy.

On May 1, Jackson's four divisions hit the Federals hard and Hooker pulled his army back around the Chancellor house, deeper into the wilderness. That evening Generals Lee and Jackson met around a small fire at a crossroads in the woods and concocted the most daring plan of attack of the war. The next day Jackson marched his entire corps on small back roads completely across the front of the enemy army without serious detection. Nearly 21,000 men in a battle line a mile and half long were prepared to step off through the woods against the unsuspecting Union 11th Corps on the Yankee army's right flank.

"Shortly before 5 P.M., Major Sandie Pendleton dismounted. The line of battle was formed, he announced. Jackson quickly rode to high ground at the Luckett farm. A cluster of officers joined him. Jackson looked around. Familiar faces from VMI stared back. In yesteryear they had been cadets and fellow professors. Now they were division commanders, brigadiers, regimental colonels—seventeen in all—and they were still seeking to please their sometimes strange but always inspiring leader. Emotion overtook Jackson. 'The Institute will be heard from today,' he said." [11]

The avalanche of Confederate veterans fell on the unsuspecting Yankee troops and the rout of the 11th Corps was complete. Because the attack began so late in the day, darkness brought a halt to continued movement. During the night, Stonewall Jackson and several of his staff rode out in front of the confused Confederate lines to gather information about enemy dispositions. Nervous Southern pickets, thinking that the returning general's entourage was a Yankee column, opened fire in the dark, and Stonewall Jackson was struck by three .57 caliber balls in the left shoulder and arm and right hand. Ten of the nineteen men with Jackson were hit; three aides and Keith Boswell were killed.

After a harrowing night of being carried, dropped, and hauled in an ambulance through the woods, Jackson was taken to the corps hospital where Dr. McGuire amputated his arm. The next day proved to be the second bloodiest day of the war as the two armies fired into each other on the wilderness battlefield, but Jackson remained under the ministrations of his physicians. The general sent Lt. Morrison, his brother-in-law, to Richmond to bring Anna. He received a dispatch from General Lee in which he expressed his regret at Jackson's wounding and concluded, "I should have chosen for the good of the country to have been disabled in your stead . . . I congratulate you upon the victory which is due to your skill and energy." After the message was read to him he turned his face away and replied, "General Lee is very kind, but he should give the praise to God."

Jackson was taken to a small office building on the grounds of the Chandler house at Guiney Station, twenty-seven miles from the fighting. Anna was not able to reach his side for five days after he was wounded. Hours after she finally arrived, she was summoned to his side:

> Oh, the fearful change since I had last seen him! It required
> the strongest effort of which I was capable to maintain my

self-control. When he left me on the morning of the 29th, going forth so cheerfully and bravely to the call of duty, he was in the full flush of vigorous manhood, and during that last, blessed visit, I never saw him look so handsome, so happy, and so noble. *Now*, his fearful wounds, his mutilated arm, the scratches upon his face, and, above all, the desperate pneumonia, which was flushing his cheeks, oppressing his breathing, and benumbing his senses, wring my soul with such grief and anguish as it had never before experienced. He had to be aroused to speak to me, and expressed much joy and thankfulness at seeing me; but he was too much affected by morphia to resist stupor, and soon seemed to lose the consciousness of my presence, except when I spoke or ministered to him. From the time I reached him he was too ill to notice or talk much, and he lay most of the time in a semi-conscious state; but when aroused, he recognized those about him and consciousness would return. Soon after I entered his room he was impressed by the woeful anxiety and sadness betrayed in my face, and said:

"My darling, you must cheer up, and not wear a long face. I love cheerfulness and brightness in a sick-room."

And he requested me to speak distinctly, as he wished to hear every word I said. Whenever he awakened from his stupor, he always had some endearing words to say to me, such as,

"My darling, you are very much loved."

"You are one of the most precious little wives in the world."

He told me he knew I would be glad to take his place, but God knew what was best for us. Thinking it would cheer him more than anything else to see the baby in whom he had so delighted, I proposed several times to bring her to his bedside, but he always said,

"Not yet; wait till I feel better."

He was invariably patient, never uttering a murmur or complaint.

On Saturday afternoon, in the hope of soothing him, I proposed reading some selections from the Psalms. At first he replied that he was suffering too much to listen, but very soon he added:

"Yes, we must never refuse that. Get the Bible and read them."

As night approached, and he grew more wearied, he requested me to sing to him—asking that the songs should be the most spiritual that could be selected. My brother Joseph assisted me in singing a few hymns, and at my husband's request we concluded with the 51st Psalm in verse: "Show pity, Lord; O Lord, forgive." The singing had a quieting effect, and he seemed to rest in perfect peace.

He asked to see his chaplain, Mr. Lacy, but his respiration being now very difficult, it was not thought prudent for him to converse, and an attempt was made to dissuade him. But he was so persistent that it was deemed best to gratify him. When Mr. Lacy entered he inquired of him if he was trying to further those views of Sabbath observance of which he had spoken to him. Upon being assured that this was being done, he expressed much gratification, and talked for some time upon that subject— his last care and effort for the church of Christ being to secure the sanctification of the Lord's day.

Mr. Lacy was truly a spiritual comforter and help to me in those dark and agonizing days. Often when I was called out of the sick-chamber to my little nursling, before returning we would meet together, and, bowing down before the throne of grace, pour out our hearts to God to spare that precious, useful life, *if consistent with His will;* for without this condition, which the Saviour himself enjoins, we dared not plead for that life, infinitely dearer, as it was, than my own.

I well knew that death to him was but the opening of the gates of pearl into the ineffable glories of heaven; but I had heard him say that, although he was willing and ready to die at any moment that God might call him, still he would prefer to have a few hours' preparation before entering into the presence of his Maker and Redeemer.

I therefore felt it to be my duty to gratify his desire. He now appeared to be fast sinking into unconsciousness, but he heard my voice and understood me better than others, and God gave me the strength and composure to hold a last sacred interview with him, in which I tried to impress upon him his situation, and learn his dying wishes.

When I told him the doctors thought he would soon be in heaven, he did not seem to comprehend it, and showed no surprise or concern. But upon repeating it, and asking him if he was willing for God to do with him according to His own will, he looked at me calmly and intelligently, and said,

"Yes, I prefer it, I prefer it."

I then told him that before that day was over he would be with the blessed Saviour in His glory. With perfect distinctness and intelligence, he said,

"I will be an infinite gainer to be translated."

He now sank rapidly into unconsciousness, murmuring disconnected words occasionally, but all at once he spoke out very cheerfully and distinctly the beautiful sentence which has become immortal as his last:

"Let us cross over the river, and rest under the shade of the trees."

The thirty-nine-year-old Stonewall Jackson was mourned throughout the Confederacy, but his testimony and example lived on in the lives and memories of those who knew him and with many who have studied his life. None knew or loved him more than his beloved Anna, who cherished his memory and left a record of some of his correspondence for the edification of posterity and the Glory of God.

THE MAXIMS OF STONEWALL JACKSON

General Jackson began keeping a book of maxims when a cadet at West Point and added principles that he thought would help him in the years that followed. They reveal much about his character and his wisdom.

STONEWALL JACKSON'S MAXIMS

Reminders for Accumulating Friends

1. A man is known by the company he keeps.
2. Be cautious in your selection.
3. There is danger of catching the habits of your associates.
4. Seek those who are intelligent & virtuous & if possible those who are a little above you, especially in moral excellence.

5. It is not desirable to have a large no. of intimate friends. You may have many acquaintances but few intimate friends. If you have one who is what he should be, you are comparatively happy. That friendship may be at once fond and lasting, there must not only be equal virtue in each party, but virtue of the same kind: not only the same end must be proposed but the same means must be approved.

Social Communication

1. Ascertain in your conversation as well as you can wherein the skill & excellence of the individual lies & put him upon his favorite subject. Every person will of his own accord fall to talking on his favorite subject or topic if you will follow and not attempt to lead him.

2. If you seek to improve in the greatest degree from the conversation of another, allow him to take his own course. If called upon, converse in turn upon your favorite topic.

3. Never interrupt another but hear him out. There are certain individuals from whom little information is to be desired such as use [of] wanton, obscene or profane language.

4. If you speak in company, speak late.

5. Let your words be as few as will express the sense you wish to convey & above all let what you say be true.

6. Do not suffer your feelings to betray you into too much vehemence or earnestness or to being overbearing.

7. Avoid triumphing over an antagonist.

8. Never engross the whole conversation to yourself.

9. Sit or stand still while another is speaking to you—[do] not dig the earth with your foot nor take your knife from your pocket & pare your nails nor other such actions.

10. Never anticipate for another to help him out. It is time enough for you to make corrections after he has concluded, if any are necessary. It is impolite to interrupt another in his remarks.

11. Say as little of yourself & friends as possible.

12. Make it a rule never to accuse without due consideration any body or association of men.

13. Never try to appear more wise or learned than the rest of the company. Not that you should affect ignorance, but endeavor to remain within your own proper sphere. Let ease & gracefulness be the standard by which you form your estimation (taken from etiquette).

Guidelines for Good Behavior

1. Through life let your principal object be the discharge of duty: if anything conflicts with it, adhere to the former and sacrifice the latter.

   Be sociable—speak to all who speak to you and those whose acquaintance you do not wish to avoid, hesitate not to notice them first.

   When in company, do not endeavor to monopolize all the conversation unless such monopolization appears necessary, but be content with listening and gaining information, yet converse rather than suffer conversation to draw to a close unnecessarily.

2. Disregard public opinion when it interferes with your duty. After you have formed an acquaintance with an individual, never allow it to draw to a close without a cause.

3. Endeavor to be at peace with all men. Never speak disrespectfully of any one without a cause.

4. Endeavor to do well every thing which you undertake through preference.

5. Spare no effort to suppress selfishness unless that effort would entail sorrow.

6. Sacrifice your life rather than your word. Be temperate. Eat too little rather than too much.

7. Let your conduct towards men have some uniformity.

   Temperance—Eat not to dullness, drink not to elevation.

   Silence—Speak not but what may benefit others or yourself: avoid trifling conversation.

   Order—Let all things have their places: let each part of your business have its time.

8. Resolution—Resolve to perform what you ought: perform without fail what you resolve.

   Frugality—Make no expense but to do good to others or yourself: i.e., waste nothing.

   Industry—Lose no time; be always employed in something useful; cut off all unnecessary actions.

   Sincerity—Use no hurtful deceit: think innocently and justly, and if you speak, speak accordingly.

Justice—Wrong none by doing injuries or omitting the benefits that are your duty.

Moderation—Avoid extremes: forbear resenting injuries so much as you think they deserve.

Cleanliness—Tolerate no uncleanliness in body, clothes, or habitation.

Tranquility—Be not disturbed at trifles nor at accidents common or unavoidable.

Chastity

Humility

"You may be what ever you will resolve to be."

Motives to Action (Viz)

1. Regard to your own happiness.
2. Regard for the family to which you belong.
3. Strive to attain a very great elevation of character.
4. Fix upon a high standard of character.
5. Fix upon a high standard of action.
6. It is man's highest interest not to violate or attempt to violate the rules which infinite wisdom has laid down.

Politeness & Good-breeding

Good breeding or true politeness is the art of showing men by external signs the internal regard we have for them.

It arises from good sense improved by good company.

It must be acquired by practice and not by books.

Be kind, condescending, & affable.

Anyone who has any thing to say to a fellow human being to say it with a kind feeling & sincere desire to please & this when ever it is done will atone for much awkwardness in the manner of expression.

Forced complaisance is fopping [foppishness?] & affected easiness is ridiculous.

Good breeding is opposed to selfishness, vanity, or pride.

Endeavor to please without hardly allowing it to be perceived.

A p p e n d i x   B

STONEWALL JACKSON
ON THE CHURCH

General Jackson corresponded with his pastor throughout the war and they reveal his continued interest in the spiritual health of the church and views on the church's responsibility to the army. One such letter touched upon the importance of army chaplains:

> My views are summed up in these few words: Each Christian branch of the Church should send into the army some of its most prominent ministers, who are distinguished for their piety, talents, and zeal; and such ministers should labor to produce concert of action among chaplains and Christians in the army. These ministers should give special attention to preaching to regiments which are without chaplains, and induce them to take steps to get chaplains; to let the regiments name the denomination from which

they desire chaplains selected; and then to see that suitable chaplains are secured. A bad selection of a chaplain may prove a curse instead of a blessing. If a few prominent ministers thus connected with each army would cordially co-operate, I believe that glorious fruits would be the result. Denominational distinctions should be kept out of view, and not touched upon; and, as a general rule, I do not think that a chaplain who would preach denominational sermons should be in the army. His congregation is his regiment, and it is composed of persons of various denominations. I would like to see no questions asked in the army as to what denomination a chaplain belongs; but let the question be, "Does he preach the Gospel?" The neglect of spiritual interests in the army may be partially seen in the fact that not half of my regiments have chaplains.

BIBLIOGRAPHICAL NOTES

Because this book is primarily about the relationship between General Stonewall Jackson and his wife Mary Anna, the military campaigns and battles are just briefly summarized to give context to the letters. Of necessity, the roles of other prominent leaders, both Northern and Southern, are mostly left out. Also, General Jackson wrote letters to many other people, most of which could not be included in this book.

Stonewall Jackson was a man with weaknesses and failures, which hardly appear in this text but which were real and sometimes had more negative consequences than indicated here. There are several excellent biographies of Stonewall Jackson which show him in a more complete form.

The first official biography of the general, *The Life and Campaigns of Stonewall Jackson* by Robert Lewis Dabney, is a gold mine of first-person observations by his close friend and adjutant general. It offers the immediacy of direct observation and intimacy but lacks the accuracy and perspective that the passing of time provides historians.

Mary Anna Jackson's *The Life and Letters of Stonewall Jackson*, from which this book is primarily derived, is a warm and loving biography by his wife. It relies heavily on Dabney for the military operations but provides a wonderful personal account of Jackson's family life.

The best overall account of Jackson's life and career is the superb biography by James I. Robertson, *Stonewall Jackson, The Man, The Soldier, The Legend* (Macmillan Publishing, New York, 1997). For the first time since Anna Jackson's biography, an historian has taken the general's Christian faith seriously, described his family and church life with sympathy and understanding, and has brought a lifetime of research, writing, and expertise concerning the battles and campaigns of the eastern theater of the War Between the States to the art of biography.

ENDNOTES

Most of the unattributed quotations are from *The Life and Letters of General Thomas J. Jackson* by Mary Anna Jackson (Sprinkle Publications, Harrisonburg, Virginia, 1995).

1. Robertson, James I., *Stonewall Jackson: The Man, The Soldier, The Legend*, Macmillan Publishing, New York, 1997, p. 44.
2. Ibid., p. 149.
3. Ibid., p. 213.
4. Ibid., p. 224.
5. Ibid., p. 283.
6. Quoted in ibid., p. 323.
7. Shaw, Maurice F., *Stonewall Jackson's Surgeon Hunter Holmes McGuire: A Biography*, H.E. Howard, Inc., Lynchburg, Virginia, 1993, quoted in p. 22.

8. Dabney, Robert Lewis, D.D., *Life and Campaigns of Lieut.-Gen. Thomas J. Jackson*, Sprinkle Publications, Harrisonburg, Virginia, 1983.

9. Ibid., p. 565.

10. Quoted in Robertson, p. 628.

11. Ibid., p. 721.